Ninja Foodi
2-Basket Air Fryer
Cookbook with Pictures

Simple & Delicious 2-Basket Air Fryer Recipes for Beginners and Advanced Users

Julia Adamo

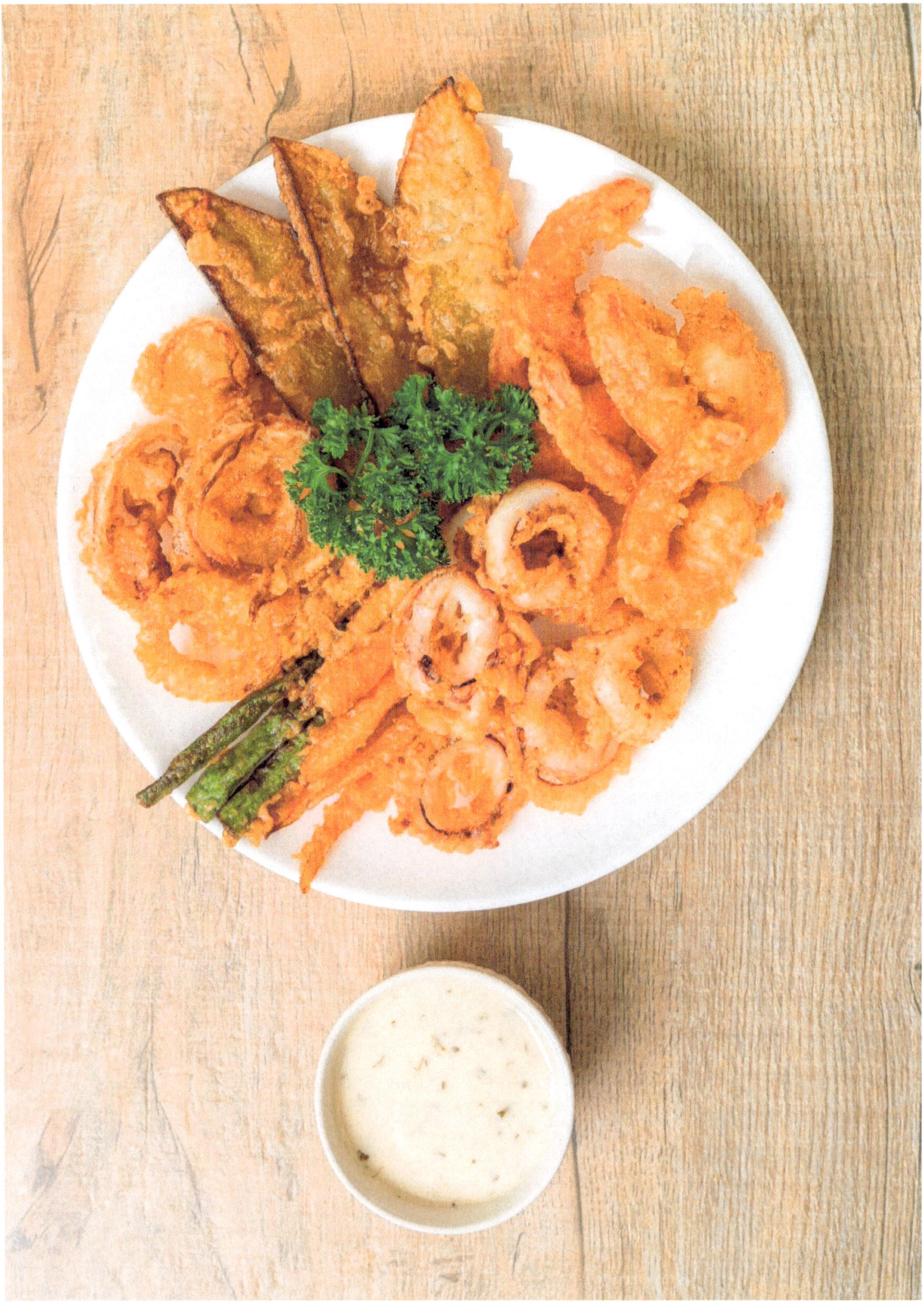

Table of Contents

Introduction 5
Main Functions of Ninja Foodi 2-Basket Air Fryer 6

User's Guide of Ninja Foodi 2-Basket Air Fryer 6

Cleaning & Maintaining Tips 7

Breakfast Recipes 8
Sausage with Eggs 8

Bacon and Egg Omelet 8

Sweet Potatoes Hash 9

Morning Patties 10

Banana and Raisins Muffins 10

Yellow Potatoes with Eggs 11

Egg with Baby Spinach 12

Breakfast Bacon 12

Biscuit Balls 13

Pumpkin Muffins 14

Cinnamon Toasts 14

Snacks and Appetizers Recipes 16
Cheddar Quiche 16

Blueberries Muffins 16

Strawberries and Walnuts Muffins 17

Dijon Cheese Sandwich 18

Peppered Asparagus 18

Parmesan French Fries 19

Spicy Chicken Tenders 19

Stuffed Bell Peppers 20

Potato Tater Tots 21

Chicken Tenders 21

Onion Rings 22

Chicken Crescent Wraps 23

Vegetables and Sides Recipes 24
Green Beans with Baked Potatoes 24

Brussels Sprouts 24

Lime Glazed Tofu 25

Kale and Spinach Chips 25

Zucchini with Stuffing 26

Cheesy Potatoes with Asparagus 27

Stuffed Tomatoes 27

Quinoa Patties 28

Curly Fries 29

Fried Artichoke Hearts 30

Falafel 30

Air Fried Okra 31

Fried Olives 32

Fish and Seafood Recipes 33
Two-Way Salmon 33

Salmon with Green Beans 33

Fish Sandwich 34

Codfish with Herb Vinaigrette 35

Buttered Mahi-Mahi 35

Beer Battered Fish Fillet 36

Salmon with Broccoli and Cheese 37

Salmon with Coconut 37

Smoked Salmon 38

Salmon with Fennel Salad 38

Seafood Shrimp Omelet 39
Crusted Tilapia.................................... 40
Salmon Nuggets.................................. 40
Savory Salmon Fillets 41
Fried Lobster Tails 42
Crusted Shrimp.................................... 42

Poultry Mains Recipes 44

Cornish Hen with Baked Potatoes 44
Chicken & Broccoli............................... 44
General Tso's Chicken.......................... 45
Spicy Chicken 46
Crumbed Chicken Katsu 47
Pickled Chicken Fillets 47
Chicken Breast Strips........................... 48
Balsamic Duck Breast 49
Chili Chicken Wings 49
Air Fried Turkey Breast 50
Veggie Stuffed Chicken Breasts 51
Chicken Wings 51
Spice-Rubbed Chicken Pieces 52
Chicken Potatoes................................. 52
Yummy Chicken Breasts 53
Chicken Leg Piece 54
Cheddar-Stuffed Chicken..................... 54

Beef, Pork, and Lamb Recipes 55

Beef & Broccoli 55
Short Ribs & Root Vegetables................ 55
Pork Chops.. 56
Glazed Steak Recipe 56
Beef Ribs I 57

Beef Ribs II... 57
Chinese BBQ Pork................................ 58
Pork Chops with Brussels Sprouts 59
Chipotle Beef 59
Turkey and Beef Meatballs 60
Pork with Green Beans and Potatoes 61
Zucchini Pork Skewers 61
Air Fryer Meatloaves 62
Spicy Lamb Chops 63

Dessert Recipes 64

Mini Blueberry Pies 64
Lemony Sweet Twists........................... 64
Biscuit Doughnuts................................ 65
Fudge Brownies................................... 65
Walnuts Fritters................................... 66
Air Fryer Sweet Twists.......................... 67
Chocolate Chip Cake 67
Apple Hand Pies 68
Pumpkin Muffins.................................. 69
Chocolate Chip Muffins 69
Apple Crisp... 70
Zesty Cranberry Scones 71

4-Week Meal Plan 72

Week 1 72
Week 2 73
Week 3 74
Week 4 75

Conclusion 76

Introduction

If you live on a busy street and can't even slow down for a meal though the temptation of food is always calling, an air fryer is your best and most convenient remedy. With faster cooking than traditional ovens, it lowers your risk of foodborne illnesses and burns from hot oils. The Ninja 2-Basket Air Fryer is a smart purchase for a busy chef, allowing you to cook well-balanced meals fast. With dozens of recipes to choose from, this quick guide will help you become a culinary ninja. While you're cooking, feel confident knowing that your food is being cooked with less oil than traditional ovens.

The Ninja Foodi 2-Basket Air Fryer has good features. It's among the most popular air fryers in the industry today and it's affordable. The Ninja Foodi 2-Basket Air Fryer has a lot of great features! It comes with a control panel with an adjustable temperature setting and a digital timer. Additionally, it is simple to clean surface with non-stick. It also has a capacity to be washed in dishwashing items.

The Ninja Foodi 2-Basket Air Fryer from the Ninja Foodi family is advanced and multifunctional. The stainless steel air fryer has a large cooking capacity. It can serve the whole family. The cooking basket is equipped with nonstick ceramic coating and long handles for ease of use. The Ninja Foodi 2-Basket Air Fryer is unique because it has two separate cooking baskets for cooking different foods at the same time.

The Ninja Foodi 2-Basket Air Fryer operates on dual-zone technology. It lets you cook multiple dishes simultaneously in two different baskets. This also allows for customizing the time and temperature for both cooking zones as per your desire. The cooking zones are separated by temperature controller units and cyclonic fans to evenly distribute the heat in the cooking basket. This feature ensures that both cooking zones end their cooking on the same time. The Ninja Foodi 2-Basket Air Fryer cooks your favorite fried food in a healthier way, using 75% to 80% less fat and oil as compared to the traditional method. It prepares your food so it still tastes and feels fresh.

Main Functions of Ninja Foodi 2-Basket Air Fryer

The new addition in the significant variety in air fryers is the Ninja Foodi 2-Basket Air Fryer. This appliance is a multifunctional kitchen tool that can cook two different foods with the same or different settings. It is incomparable to traditional air fryers, which usually have one basket.

This air fryer allows you to cook two different items at the same time, saving you time by cooking food in batches. The oven has a smart finish feature so both items of food are cooked at the same time. This air fryer makes crispy food by removing the moisture from food.

The 6-in-1 air fryer has functions as following:

Max Crisp: This function will help you get the same result of grilling on a gas stove. You can broil your food just like a barbeque grill. This feature on a stovetop is great for frozen fried foods. Using this function, you can add extra crunch and crispiness to your food.

Air Fry: This function allows you to fry your favorite food with minimal fats and oil. That's better for your health than traditional cooking methods. Air frying results in your food being crunchy, crispy with a nice exterior, soft and moist with a special effect on the inside. You can cook meals without frying them, but the food will still have a taste and texture. The "air fry" function will help you cook foods without changing the taste or texture.

Roast: Increase the versatility of your air fryer by turning it into a roaster oven with one push of a button. This will help you tenderize meat, vegetables, and more to perfection! Dry cooking is a great way to add flavor and texture to food.

Reheat: This is an ideal function for warming up your leftover food. It preserves food so it tastes as good as the day before.

Dehydrate: This function is great for reducing the moisture content of food. It's especially good for dehydrating your favorite vegetables, fruits, and meat slices. A result of this can be that food can be preserved for a long time remaining edible.

Bake: The function of this gadget converts your air fryer into a convection oven. It is best for cooking your favorite cakes, biscuits, and other delectable dishes.

User's Guide of Ninja Foodi 2-Basket Air Fryer

Function Buttons

Max Crisp: This frying mode gives the food a crispy touch and can be used to melt toppings of dishes.

Air Fry: Use this mode to make crispy fried food without the need for oil.

Roast: Turn the air fryer unit into a roaster oven to cook meat and make it tender and soft.

Bake: Bake delicious desserts and cakes.

Reheat: Enables you to reheat and warm previous meals.

Dehydrate: Put this mode in order to dehydrate fruit, meats, and vegetables.

Operating buttons

Time arrows: You can easily adjust the cook time settings with the up and down arrow keys to fit your recipe needs.

Temp arrows: You can use the up and down arrow keys to adjust the temperature settings for your cooking.

Match button: This function will match the cooking zone 2 settings with cooking zone 1 settings on a large quantity of the same food or for different food cooking at the same time, temperature, and function.

Start/Stop button: This button triggers the cooking process. The cooking process can be stopped or started or resumed after selecting the appropriate time and temperature settings.

Sync button: The cooking mode in this air fryer synchronizes the cooking times of the two zones and makes sure they finish at the same time.

Power button: The button is pressed to turn on or off the function once the process is complete or fully stopped.

Standby mode: The machine goes into standby mode after 10 minutes of inactivity.

Hold mode: When the sign becomes visible, it will be in sync mode. When the cooking time of one zone is more than the other, they'll appear to be on hold until they're both at the same time.

Cleaning & Maintaining Tips

This machine is not intended to be used outdoors.

The voltage indication on the switch should match the main voltage from the switch.

Do not submerge the device in water.

Keep the electric cord away from the hot regions.

To cook with an air fryer, avoid contact with the external surface.

Put the product on a level surface.

Unplug the device after use.

Air fryers are popular because they're easy to use and take up minimal counter space. Just be sure to clean your air fryer:

Unplug the appliance before cleaning it and allow it to cool down.

You can detach the baskets from the main unit and store them aside to cool.

Once they have cooled, remove their air crisper plates and put them in the dishwasher.

Clean the air fryer basket with soapy water and avoid hard scrubbing to keep safe from scratching or damaging the nonstick coatings/layers.

If your air fryer racks are stained, use a dishwasher to clean them. If food is stuck on the rack, use a soft scrub.

Wipe the top surface of the device with a begrimed part of fabric or a diminutive damp cloth.

Give them a moment to dry and then return them to the air fryer.

Your device is now set up and ready for reuse.

Breakfast Recipes

Sausage with Eggs

Prep time: 10 minutes| **Cook time:** 13 minutes| **Serves:** 2

Ingredients:

- 4 sausage links, raw and uncooked
- 4 eggs, uncooked
- 1 tablespoon green onion
- 2 tablespoons chopped tomatoes
- Salt and black pepper, to taste
- 2 tablespoons milk, dairy
- Oil spray, for greasing

Directions:

1. Take a bowl and whisk eggs in it.
2. Then pour milk, and add the onions and tomatoes.
3. Whisk it all well.
4. Now season it with salt and black pepper.
5. Take one cake pan that fits inside the air fryer and grease it with oil spray.
6. Pour the omelet into the greased cake pan.
7. Put the cake pan inside zone 1 of the Ninja Foodie 2-Basket Air Fryer.
8. Now place the sausage link into the zone 2 basket.
9. Select BAKE for zone 1 basket and set the timer to 8-10 minutes at 300 degrees F.
10. For zone 2, select the AIR FRY button and set the timer to 12 minutes at 390 degrees F.
11. Once the cooking cycle is complete, serve by transferring it to plates.
12. Chop the sausage or cut it in round chunks and then mix it with the egg.
13. Enjoy hot as a delicious breakfast.

Serving Suggestion: Serve it with toasted bread slices.

Variation Tip: Use almond milk if you like non-dairy milk.

Per Serving: Calories 240; Fat 18.4g; Sodium 396mg; Carbs 2.8g; Fiber 0.2g; Sugar 2g; Protein 15.6g

Bacon and Egg Omelet

Prep time: 12 minutes| **Cook time:** 10 minutes| **Serves:** 2

Ingredients:

- 2 eggs, whisked
- ½ teaspoon chopped tomatoes
- Sea salt and black pepper, to taste
- 2 teaspoons almond milk
- 1 teaspoon cilantro, chopped
- 1 small green chili, chopped
- 4 strips bacon
- Oil spray, for greasing

Directions:

1. Take a bowl and whisk the eggs in it.
2. Then add the green chili, salt, black pepper, cilantro, almond milk, and chopped tomatoes.
3. Grease the ramekins with oil spray.
4. Pour this into ramekins.
5. Put the bacon in the zone 1 basket and ramekins in zone 2 basket of the Ninja Foodi 2-Basket Air Fryer.
6. Now for zone 1, set it to AIR FRY mode at 400 degrees F for 10 minutes.
7. For zone 2, set it to 350 degrees for 10 minutes in AIR FRY mode.
8. Press the Sync button and press START/STOP button so that it will finish both at the same time.
9. Once done, serve and enjoy.

Serving Suggestion: Serve it with bread slices and ketchup.

Variation Tip: Use garlic salt instead of sea salt.

Per Serving: Calories 285; Fat 21.5g; Sodium 1000mg; Carbs 2.2g; Fiber 0.1g; Sugar 1g; Protein 19.7g

Sweet Potatoes Hash

Prep time: 15 minutes| **Cook time:** 25 minutes| **Serves:** 2

Ingredients:

- 450 grams sweet potatoes
- ½ white onion, diced
- 3 tablespoons olive oil
- 1 teaspoon smoked Paprika
- ¼ teaspoon cumin
- ⅓ teaspoon ground turmeric
- ¼ teaspoon garlic salt
- 1 cup guacamole

Directions:

1. Peel and cut the potatoes into cubes.
2. Transfer the potatoes to a bowl and add oil, white onions, cumin, Paprika, turmeric, and garlic salt.
3. Put this mixture between both the baskets of the Ninja Foodie 2-Basket Air Fryer.
4. Set zone 1 to AIR FRY mode for 10 minutes at 390 degrees F.
5. Press the MATCH button for zone 2.
6. Take out the baskets and shake them well.
7. Set the timer to 15 minutes at 390 degrees F and AIR FRY again and MATCH for zone 2.
8. Once done, serve it with guacamole.

Serving Suggestion: Serve it with ketchup and omelet.

Variation Tip: Use canola oil instead of olive oil.

Per Serving: Calories 691; Fat 49.7g; Sodium 596mg; Carbs 64g; Fiber15g; Sugar 19g; Protein 8.1g

Morning Patties

Prep time: 15 minutes| **Cook time:** 13 minutes| **Serves:** 4

Ingredients:

- 1 lb. minced pork
- 1 lb. minced turkey
- 2 teaspoons dry rubbed sage
- 2 teaspoons fennel seeds
- 2 teaspoons garlic powder
- 1 teaspoon paprika
- 1 teaspoon of sea salt
- 1 teaspoon dried thyme

Directions:

1. In a mixing bowl, add turkey and pork, then mix them together.
2. Mix sage, fennel, paprika, salt, thyme, and garlic powder in a small bowl.
3. Drizzle this mixture over the meat mixture and mix well.
4. Take 2 tablespoons of this mixture at a time and roll it into thick patties.
5. Place half of the patties in Zone 1, and the other half in Zone 2, then spray them all with cooking oil.
6. Return the crisper plate to the Ninja Foodi 2-Basket Air Fryer.
7. Choose the Air Fry mode for Zone 1 and set the temperature to 390 degrees F and the time to 13 minutes.
8. Select the "MATCH" button to copy the settings for Zone 2.
9. Initiate cooking by pressing the START/STOP button.
10. Flip the patties in the drawers once cooked halfway through.
11. Serve warm and fresh.

Serving Suggestion: Serve the patties with toasted bread slices.

Variation Tip: Ground chicken or beef can also be used instead of ground pork and turkey.

Per Serving: Calories 305; Fat 25g; Sodium 532mg; Carbs 2.3g; Fiber 0.4g; Sugar 2g; Protein 18.3g

Banana and Raisins Muffins

Prep time: 20 minutes| **Cook time:** 16 minutes| **Serves:** 2

Ingredients:

- Salt, pinch
- 2 eggs, whisked
- ⅓ cup butter, melted
- 4 tablespoons almond milk
- ¼ teaspoon vanilla extract
- ½ teaspoon baking powder
- 1½ cup all-purpose flour
- 1 cup mashed bananas
- 2 tablespoons raisins

Directions:

1. Take about 4 large (one-cup sized) ramekins and layer them with muffin papers.
2. Crack the eggs in a large bowl, and whisk it all well and add vanilla extract, almond milk, baking powder, and melted butter.
3. Whisk the Ingredients: in very well.
4. Take a separate bowl and add the all-purpose flour and salt.
5. Combine the dry Ingredients: with the wet Ingredients.
6. Pour mashed bananas and raisins into the batter.
7. Mix it well to make a batter for the muffins.
8. Pour the batter into the four ramekins and divide the ramekins into the air fryer zones.
9. Set the timer for zone 1 to 16 minutes at 350 degrees F on AIR FRY mode.
10. Select the MATCH button for the zone 2 basket.
11. Check and if not done, and let it AIR FRY for one more minute.
12. Once it is done, serve.

Serving Suggestion: None

Variation Tip: None

Per Serving: Calories 727; Fat 43.1g; Sodium 366 mg; Carbs 74.4g; Fiber 4.7g; Sugar 16.1g; Protein 14.1g

Yellow Potatoes with Eggs

Prep time: 10 minutes| **Cook time:** 35 minutes| **Serves:** 2

Ingredients:

- 1 pound Dutch yellow potatoes, quartered
- 1 red bell pepper, chopped
- Salt and black pepper, to taste
- 1 green bell pepper, chopped
- 2 teaspoons olive oil
- 2 teaspoons garlic powder
- 1 teaspoon onion powder
- 1 egg
- ¼ teaspoon butter

Directions:

1. Toss together diced potatoes, green pepper, red pepper, salt, black pepper, and olive oil along with garlic powder and onion powder.
2. Put the potatoes in the zone 1 basket of the air fryer.
3. Take a ramekin and grease it with oil spray.
4. Whisk the egg in a bowl and add salt and pepper along with ½ teaspoon of butter.
5. Pour the egg into the ramekin and place it in the zone 2 basket.
6. Set the timer for zone 1 basket to 30-35 minutes at 400 degrees F at AIR FRY mode.
7. Now for zone 2, set it to AIR FRY mode at 350 degrees F for 8-10 minutes.
8. Press the Sync button and press START/STOP button so both will finish at the same time.
9. Once done, serve and enjoy.

Serving Suggestion: Serve it with sourdough toasted bread slices.

Variation Tip: Use white potatoes instead of yellow Dutch potatoes.

Per Serving: Calories 252; Fat 7.5g; Sodium 37mg; Carbs 40g; Fiber 3.9g; Sugar 7g; Protein 6.7g

Egg with Baby Spinach

Prep time: 12 minutes| **Cook time:** 12 minutes| **Serves:** 4

Ingredients:

- Nonstick spray, for greasing ramekins
- 2 tablespoons olive oil
- 6 ounces baby spinach
- 2 garlic cloves, minced
- ⅓ teaspoon kosher salt
- 6-8 large eggs
- ½ cup half and half
- Salt and black pepper, to taste
- 8 Sourdough bread slices, toasted

Directions:

1. Grease 4 ramekins with oil spray and set them aside for further use.
2. Take a skillet and heat oil in it.
3. Cook spinach for 2 minutes and add the garlic, salt and black pepper.
4. Let it simmer for 2 more minutes.
5. Once the spinach is wilted, transfer it to a plate.
6. Whisk the eggs in a small bowl.
7. Add in the spinach.
8. Whisk it well and then pour in the half and half.
9. Divide this mixture between 4 ramekins and remember not to overfill it to the top.
10. Put the ramekins in zone 1 and zone 2 baskets of the Ninja Foodie 2-Basket Air Fryer.
11. Press START/STOP button and set zone 1 to AIR FRY at 350 degrees F for 8-12 minutes.
12. Press the MATCH button for zone 2.
13. Once it's cooked and eggs are done, serve with sourdough bread slices.

Serving Suggestion: Serve it with cream cheese topping.

Variation Tip: Use plain bread slices instead of sourdough bread slices.

Per Serving: Calories 404; Fat 19.6g; Sodium 761mg; Carbs 40.1g; Fiber 2.5g; Sugar 2.5g; Protein 19.2g

Breakfast Bacon

Prep time: 10 minutes| **Cook time:** 14 minutes| **Serves:** 4

Ingredients:

- ½ lb. bacon slices

Directions:

1. Spread half of the bacon slices in each of the crisper plate evenly in a single layer.
2. Return the crisper plate to the Ninja Foodi 2-Basket Air Fryer.
3. Choose the Air Fry mode for Zone 1 and set the temperature to 390 degrees F and the time to 14 minutes.

4. Select the "MATCH" button to copy the settings for Zone 2.
5. Initiate cooking by pressing the START/STOP button.
6. Flip the crispy bacon once cooked halfway through, then resume cooking.
7. Serve.

Serving Suggestion: Serve the bacon with eggs and bread slices.

Variation Tip: Add salt and black pepper for seasoning.

Per Serving: Calories 273; Fat 22g; Sodium 517mg; Carbs 3.3g; Fiber 0.2g; Sugar 1.4g; Protein 16.1g

Biscuit Balls

Prep time: 10 minutes| **Cook time:** 18 minutes| **Serves:** 6

Ingredients:
- 1 tablespoon butter
- 2 eggs, beaten
- ¼ teaspoon pepper
- 1 can (10.2-oz) Pillsbury Buttermilk biscuits
- 2 ounces cheddar cheese, diced into ten cubes
- Cooking spray
- Egg Wash
- 1 egg
- 1 tablespoon water

Directions:
1. Place a suitable non-stick skillet over medium-high heat and cook the bacon until crispy, then place it on a plate lined with a paper towel.
2. Melt butter in the same skillet over medium heat. Beat eggs with pepper in a bowl and pour them into the skillet.
3. Stir cook for 5 minutes, then remove it from the heat.
4. Add bacon and mix well.
5. Divide the dough into 5 biscuits and slice each into 2 layers.
6. Press each biscuit into 4-inch round.
7. Add a tablespoon of the egg mixture at the center of each round and top it with a piece of cheese.
8. Carefully fold the biscuit dough around the filling and pinch the edges to seal.
9. Whisk egg with water in a small bowl and brush the egg wash over the biscuits.
10. Place half of the biscuit bombs in each of the crisper plate and spray them with cooking oil.
11. Return the crisper plate to the Ninja Foodi 2-Basket Air Fryer.
12. Choose the Air Fry mode for Zone 1 and set the temperature to 375 degrees F and the time to 14 minutes.
13. Select the "MATCH" button to copy the settings for Zone 2.
14. Initiate cooking by pressing the START/STOP button.
15. Flip the egg bombs when cooked halfway through, then resume cooking.
16. Serve warm.

Serving Suggestion: Serve the eggs balls with crispy bacon.

Variation Tip: Add dried herbs to the egg filling.

Per Serving: Calories 102; Fat 7.6g; Sodium 545mg; Carbs 1.5g; Fiber 0.4g; Sugar 0.7g; Protein 7.1g

Pumpkin Muffins

Prep time: 15 minutes| **Cook time:** 13 minutes| **Serves:** 8

Ingredients:

- ½ cup pumpkin puree
- 1 cup gluten-free oats
- ¼ cup honey
- 1 medium egg beaten
- ½ teaspoon coconut butter
- ½ tablespoon cocoa nib
- ½ tablespoon vanilla essence
- Cooking spray
- ½ teaspoon nutmeg

Directions:

1. Add oats, honey, eggs, pumpkin puree, coconut butter, cocoa nibs, vanilla essence, and nutmeg to a bowl and mix well until smooth.
2. Divide the batter into two 4-cup muffin trays, greased with cooking spray.
3. Place one mini muffin tray in each of the two crisper plates.
4. Return the crisper plates to the Ninja Foodi 2-Basket Air Fryer.
5. Choose the Air Fry mode for Zone 1 and set the temperature to 375 degrees F and the time to 13 minutes.
6. Select the "MATCH" button to copy the settings for Zone 2.
7. Initiate cooking by pressing the START/STOP button.
8. Allow the muffins to cool, then serve.

Serving Suggestion: Serve the muffins with a hot coffee.

Variation Tip: Add raisins and nuts to the batter before baking.

Per Serving: Calories 209; Fat 7.5g; Sodium 321mg; Carbs 34.1g; Fiber 4g; Sugar 3.8g; Protein 4.3g

Cinnamon Toasts

Prep time: 15 minutes| **Cook time:** 8 minutes| **Serves:** 4

Ingredients:

- 4 pieces of bread
- 2 tablespoons butter
- 2 eggs, beaten
- 1 pinch salt
- 1 pinch cinnamon ground
- 1 pinch nutmeg ground
- 1 pinch ground clove
- 1 teaspoon icing sugar

Directions:

1. Add two eggs to a mixing bowl and stir cinnamon, nutmeg, ground cloves, and salt, then whisk well.
2. Spread butter on both sides of the bread slices and cut them into thick strips.

3. Dip the breadsticks in the egg mixture and place them in the two crisper plates.
4. Return the crisper plates to the Ninja Foodi 2-Basket Air Fryer.
5. Choose the Air Fry mode for Zone 1 and set the temperature to 390 degrees F and the time to 8 minutes.
6. Select the "MATCH" button to copy the settings for Zone 2.
7. Initiate cooking by pressing the START/STOP button.
8. Flip the French toast sticks when cooked halfway through.
9. Serve.

Serving Suggestion: Serve the toasted with chocolate syrup or Nutella spread.

Variation Tip: Use crushed cornflakes for breading to have extra crispiness.

Per Serving: Calories 199; Fat 11.1g; Sodium 297mg; Carbs 14.9g; Fiber 1g; Sugar 2.5g; Protein 9.9g

Snacks and Appetizers Recipes

Cheddar Quiche

Prep time: 10 minutes| **Cook time:** 12 minutes| **Serves:** 2

Ingredients:

- 4 eggs, organic
- 1¼ cup heavy cream
- Salt, pinch
- ½ cup broccoli florets
- ½ cup Cheddar cheese, shredded and for sprinkling

Directions:

1. Take a Pyrex pitcher and crack two eggs into it.
2. Fill it with heavy cream, about half the way up.
3. Add in the salt and then the broccoli.
4. Pour the mixture into two quiche dishes, and top it with shredded Cheddar cheese.
5. Divide it into both zones of the baskets.
6. For zone 1, set the time to 10-12 minutes at 325 degrees F on AIR FRY mode.
7. Select the MATCH button for the zone 2 basket.
8. Once done, serve hot.

Serving Suggestion: Serve with herbs as a topping.

Variation Tip: Use spinach instead of broccoli florets.

Per Serving: Calories 454; Fat 40g; Sodium 406mg; Carbs 4.2g; Fiber 0.6g; Sugar 1.3 g; Protein 20g

Blueberries Muffins

Prep time: 15 minutes| **Cook time:** 15 minutes| **Serves:** 2

Ingredients:

- Salt, 1 pinch
- 2 eggs
- ⅓ cup sugar
- ⅓ cup vegetable oil
- 4 tablespoons water
- 1 teaspoon lemon zest
- ¼ teaspoon vanilla extract
- ½ teaspoon baking powder
- 1 cup all-purpose flour
- 1 cup blueberries

Directions:

1. Take 4 ramekins that are oven safe and layer them with muffin papers.
2. Take a bowl and whisk the egg, sugar, oil, water, vanilla extract, and lemon zest in.
3. Whisk it all very well.

4. In a separate bowl, mix the flour, baking powder, and salt.
5. Add the dry Ingredients: slowly to the wet Ingredients.
6. Pour the batter into the ramekins and top with blueberries.
7. Divide them between both zones of the Ninja Foodi 2-Basket Air Fryer.
8. Set the time for zone 1 to 15 minutes at 350 degrees F on AIR FRY mode.
9. Select the MATCH button for the zone 2 basket.
10. Check if not done, and let it AIR FRY for one more minute.
11. Once it is done, serve.

Serving Suggestion: Serve it with whipped cream topping.

Variation Tip: Use butter instead of vegetable oil.

Per Serving: Calories 781; Fat 41.6g; Sodium 143mg; Carbs 92.7g; Fiber 3.5g; Sugar41.2 g; Protein 0g

Strawberries and Walnuts Muffins

Prep time: 15 minutes| **Cook time:** 15 minutes| **Serves:** 2

Ingredients:

- Salt, pinch
- 2 eggs, whisked
- ⅓ cup maple syrup
- ⅓ cup coconut oil
- 4 tablespoons water
- 1 teaspoon orange zest
- ¼ teaspoon vanilla extract
- ½ teaspoon baking powder
- 1 cup all-purpose flour
- 1 cup strawberries, finely chopped
- ⅓ cup walnuts, chopped and roasted

Directions:

1. Layer 4 ramekins with muffin paper.
2. Add egg, maple syrup, oil, water, vanilla extract, and orange zest to a bowl and mix well.
3. In a separate bowl, mix flour, baking powder, and salt.
4. Add the dry Ingredients: slowly to the wet Ingredients.
5. Pour the batter into the ramekins and top with strawberries and walnuts.
6. Divide the ramekins into both zones. For zone 1, set to AIR FRY mode at 350 degrees F for 15 minutes.
7. Select the MATCH button for the zone 2 basket.
8. Check and if not done, let it AIR FRY for one more minute.
9. Once done, serve.

Serving Suggestion: Serve it with coffee.

Variation Tip: Use vegetable oil instead of coconut oil.

Per Serving: Calories 897; Fat 53.9g; Sodium 148mg; Carbs 92g; Fiber 4.7g; Sugar 35.6 g; Protein 17.5g

Dijon Cheese Sandwich

Prep time: 10 minutes| **Cook time:** 10 minutes| **Serves:** 2

Ingredients:

- 4 large slices sourdough, whole grain
- 4 tablespoons Dijon mustard
- 1½ cup grated sharp Cheddar cheese
- 2 teaspoons green onion, green part chopped off
- 2 tablespoons butter melted

Directions:

1. Brush the melted butter on one side of all the bread slices.
2. Spread Dijon mustard on the other side of the slices.
3. Top the 2 bread slices with Cheddar cheese and top it with green onions.
4. Cover with the remaining two slices to make two sandwiches.
5. Place one sandwich in each basket of the air fryer.
6. Turn to AIR FRY mode for zone 1 basket at 350 degrees F for 10 minutes.
7. Use the MATCH button for zone 2.
8. Once it's done, serve.

Serving Suggestion: Serve with tomato soup.

Variation Tip: Use oil spray instead of butter.

Per Serving: Calories 617; Fat 38g; Sodium 1213mg; Carbs 40.8g; Fiber 5g; Sugar 5.6g; Protein 29.5g

Peppered Asparagus

Prep time: 10 minutes| **Cook time:** 16 minutes| **Serves:** 6

Ingredients:

- 1 bunch asparagus, trimmed
- Avocado or Olive Oil
- Himalayan salt, to taste
- Black pepper, to taste

Directions:

1. Divide the asparagus in the two crisper plate.
2. Toss the asparagus with salt, black pepper, and oil.
3. Return the crisper plate to the Ninja Foodi 2-Basket Air Fryer.
4. Choose the Air Fry mode for Zone 1 and set the temperature to 390 degrees F and the time to 16 minutes.
5. Select the "MATCH" button to copy the settings for Zone 2.
6. Initiate cooking by pressing the START/STOP button.
7. Serve warm.

Serving Suggestion: Serve with mayonnaise or cream cheese dip.

Variation Tip: Use panko crumbs for breading to have extra crispiness.

Per Serving: Calories 163; Fat 11.5g; Sodium 918mg; Carbs 8.3g; Fiber 4.2g; Sugar 0.2g; Protein 7.4g

Parmesan French Fries

Prep time: 10 minutes| **Cook time:** 20 minutes| **Serves:** 6

Ingredients:

- 3 medium russet potatoes
- 2 tablespoons parmesan cheese
- 2 tablespoons fresh parsley, chopped
- 1 tablespoon olive oil
- Salt, to taste

Directions:

1. Wash the potatoes and pass them through the fries' cutter to get ¼-inch-thick fries.
2. Place the fries in a colander and drizzle salt on top.
3. Leave these fries for 10 minutes, then rinse.
4. Toss the potatoes with parmesan cheese, oil, salt, and parsley in a bowl.
5. Divide the potatoes into the two crisper plates.
6. Return the crisper plates to the Ninja Foodi 2-Basket Air Fryer.
7. Choose the Air Fry mode for Zone 1 and set the temperature to 360 degrees F and the time to 20 minutes.
8. Select the "MATCH" button to copy the settings for Zone 2.
9. Initiate cooking by pressing the START/STOP button.
10. Toss the chips once cooked halfway through, then resume cooking.
11. Serve warm.

Serving Suggestion: Serve with tomato ketchup, Asian coleslaw, or creamed cabbage.

Variation Tip: Toss fries with black pepper for change of taste.

Per Serving: Calories 307; Fat 8.6g; Sodium 510mg; Carbs 22.2g; Fiber 1.4g; Sugar 13g; Protein 33.6g

Spicy Chicken Tenders

Prep time: 15 minutes| **Cook time:** 12 minutes| **Serves:** 2

Ingredients:

- 2 large eggs, whisked
- 2 tablespoons lemon juice
- Salt and black pepper
- 1 pound chicken tenders
- 1 cup Panko bread crumbs
- ½ cup Italian bread crumbs
- 1 teaspoon smoked Paprika
- ¼ teaspoon garlic powder
- ¼ teaspoon onion powder
- ½ cup fresh grated Parmesan cheese

Directions:

1. Take a bowl and whisk the eggs and set aside.
2. In a large bowl, add lemon juice, Paprika, salt, black pepper, garlic powder, onion powder
3. In a separate bowl, mix Panko bread crumbs, Italian bread crumbs, and Parmesan cheese.
4. Dip the chicken tenders in the spice mixture and coat well.
5. Let the tenders sit for 1 hour.
6. Dip each tender into the egg mixture and then into the bread crumbs.
7. Line both the baskets of the air fryer with parchment paper.
8. Divide the tenders between the baskets.
9. Set zone 1 basket to AIR FRY mode at 350 degrees F for 12 minutes.
10. Select the MATCH button for the zone 2 basket.
11. Once it's done, serve.

Serving Suggestion: Serve it with ketchup.

Variation Tip: Use mild Paprika instead of smoked Paprika.

Per Serving: Calories 836; Fat 36g; Sodium 1307 mg; Carbs 31.3g; Fiber 2.5g; Sugar 3.3 g; Protein 95.3g

Stuffed Bell Peppers

Prep time: 25 minutes| **Cook time:** 16 minutes| **Serves:** 3

Ingredients:

- 6 large bell peppers
- 1½ cups cooked rice
- 2 cups Cheddar cheese

Directions:

1. Cut the bell peppers in half lengthwise and remove all the seeds.
2. Fill the cavity of each bell pepper with cooked rice.
3. Divide the bell peppers into the two zones of the air fryer baskets.
4. Set the time for zone 1 for 200 degrees F for 10 minutes on AIR FRY mode.
5. Select MATCH button of zone 2 basket.
6. Take out the baskets and sprinkle cheese on top.
7. Set the time for zone 1 for 200 degrees for 6 more minutes on AIR FRY.
8. Select MATCH button of zone 2 basket.
9. Once it's done, serve.

Serving Suggestion: Serve it mashed potatoes.

Variation Tip: You can use any cheese you like.

Per Serving: Calories 605; Fat 26g; Sodium 477mg; Carbs 68.3g; Fiber 4g; Sugar 12.5g; Protein 25.6 g

Potato Tater Tots

Prep time: 10 minutes| **Cook time:** 27 minutes| **Serves:** 4

Ingredients:

- 2 potatoes, peeled
- ½ teaspoon Cajun seasoning
- Olive oil cooking spray
- Sea salt to taste

Directions:

1. Boil water in a cooking pot and cook potatoes in it for 15 minutes.
2. Drain and leave the potatoes to cool in a bowl.
3. Grate these potatoes and toss them with Cajun seasoning.
4. Make small tater tots out of this mixture.
5. Divide them into the two crisper plates and spray them with cooking oil.
6. Return the crisper plates to the Ninja Foodi 2-Basket Air Fryer.
7. Choose the Air Fry mode for Zone 1 and set the temperature to 375 degrees F and the time to 27 minutes.
8. Select the "MATCH" button to copy the settings for Zone 2.
9. Initiate cooking by pressing the START/STOP button.
10. Flip them once cooked halfway through, and resume cooking.
11. Serve warm.

Serving Suggestion: Serve with ketchup, mayonnaise, or cream cheese dip.

Variation Tip: Use crushed cornflakes for breading to have extra crispiness.

Per Serving: Calories 185; Fat 11g; Sodium 355mg; Carbs 21g; Fiber 5.8g; Sugar 3g; Protein 4.7g

Chicken Tenders

Prep time: 15 minutes| **Cook time:** 12 minutes| **Serves:** 3

Ingredients:

- 1 pound chicken tenders
- Salt and black pepper, to taste
- 1 cup Panko bread crumbs
- 2 cups Italian bread crumbs
- 1 cup Parmesan cheese
- 2 eggs
- Oil spray, for greasing

Directions:

1. Sprinkle the tenders with salt and black pepper.
2. In a medium bowl mix the Panko bread crumbs with Italian bread crumbs.
3. Add salt, pepper, and Parmesan cheese.
4. Crack two eggs into a bowl.
5. Dip the chicken tenders into the eggs and then into the bread crumbs and spray with oil spray.

6. Line both of the baskets of the air fryer with parchment paper.
7. Divide the tenders between the baskets of Ninja Foodi 2-Basket Air Fryer.
8. Set zone 1 basket to AIR FRY mode at 350 degrees F for 12 minutes.
9. Select the MATCH button for the zone 2 basket.
10. Once it's done, serve.

Serving Suggestion: Serve it with ranch or ketchup.

Variation Tip: Use Italian seasoning instead of Italian bread crumbs.

Per Serving: Calories 558; Fat 23.8g; Sodium 872mg; Carbs 20.9g; Fiber 1.7 g; Sugar 2.2 g; Protein 63.5g

Onion Rings

Prep time: 10 minutes| **Cook time:** 22 minutes| **Serves:** 4

Ingredients:

- ¾ cup all-purpose flour
- 1 teaspoon salt
- 1 large onion, cut into rings
- ½ cup cornstarch
- 2 teaspoons baking powder
- 1 cup low-fat milk
- 1 egg
- 1 cup bread crumbs
- ⅛ teaspoon paprika
- Cooking spray
- ⅛ teaspoon garlic powder

Directions:

1. Mix flour with baking powder, cornstarch, and salt in a small bowl.
2. First, coat the onion rings with flour mixture; set them aside.
3. Beat milk with egg, then add the remaining flour mixture into the egg.
4. Mix them well together to make a thick batter.
5. Now dip the floured onion rings into the prepared batter and coat them well.
6. Place the rings on a wire rack for 10 minutes.
7. Spread bread crumbs in a shallow bowl.
8. Coat the onion rings with breadcrumbs and shake off the excess.
9. Set the coated onion rings in the two crisper plates.
10. Spray all the rings with the cooking spray.
11. Return the crisper plate to the Ninja Foodi 2-Basket Air Fryer.
12. Choose the Air Fry mode for Zone 1 and set the temperature to 375 degrees F and the time to 22 minutes.
13. Select the "MATCH" button to copy the settings for Zone 2.
14. Initiate cooking by pressing the START/STOP button.
15. Flip once cooked halfway through, then resume cooking
16. Season the air fried onion rings with garlic powder and paprika.
17. Serve.

Serving Suggestion: Serve with tomato sauce or cream cheese dip.

Variation Tip: Use crushed cornflakes for breading to have extra crispiness.

Per Serving: Calories 229; Fat 1.9; Sodium 567mg; Carbs 1.9g; Fiber 0.4g; Sugar 0.6g; Protein 11.8g

Chicken Crescent Wraps

Prep time: 10 minutes| **Cook time:** 12 minutes| **Serves:** 6

Ingredients:

- 3 tablespoons chopped onion
- 3 garlic cloves, peeled and minced
- ¾ (8 ounces) package cream cheese
- 6 tablespoons butter
- 2 boneless chicken breasts, cubed, cooked
- 3 (10 ounces) cans refrigerated crescent roll dough

Directions:

1. Heat oil in a skillet and add onion and garlic to sauté until soft.
2. Add cooked chicken, sautéed veggies, butter, and cream cheese to a blender.
3. Blend well until smooth. Spread the crescent dough over a flat surface.
4. Slice the dough into 12 rectangles.
5. Spoon the chicken mixture at the center of each rectangle.
6. Roll the dough to wrap the mixture and form a ball.
7. Divide these balls into the two crisper plate.
8. Return the crisper plate to the Ninja Foodi 2-Basket Air Fryer.
9. Choose the Air Fry mode for Zone 1 and set the temperature to 390 degrees F and the time to 12 minutes.
10. Select the "MATCH" button to copy the settings for Zone 2.
11. Initiate cooking by pressing the START/STOP button.
12. Serve warm.

Serving Suggestion: Serve with tomato sauce or cream cheese dip.

Variation Tip: You can also prepare the filling using leftover turkey or pork.

Per Serving: Calories 100; Fat 2g; Sodium 480mg; Carbs 4g; Fiber 2g; Sugar 0g; Protein 18g

Vegetables and Sides Recipes

Green Beans with Baked Potatoes

Prep time: 15 minutes| **Cook time:** 45 minutes| **Serves:** 2

Ingredients:

- 2 cups green beans
- 2 large potatoes, cubed
- 3 tablespoons olive oil
- 1 teaspoon seasoned salt
- ½ teaspoon chili powder
- ⅙ teaspoon garlic powder
- ¼ teaspoon onion powder

Directions:

1. Take a large bowl and pour olive oil into it.
2. Add all the seasoning in the olive oil and whisk it well.
3. Toss the green beans in and mix well and then transfer to zone 1 basket of the air fryer.
4. Season the potatoes with the oil seasoning and add them to the zone 2 basket.
5. Press the Sync button.
6. Once the cooking cycle is complete, take out and serve.

Serving Suggestion: Serve with rice.

Variation Tip: Use canola oil instead of olive oil.

Per Serving: Calories 473; Fat 21.6g; Sodium 796mg; Carbs 66.6g; Fiber 12.9g; Sugar 6g; Protein 8.4g

Brussels Sprouts

Prep time: 15 minutes| **Cook time:** 20 minutes| **Serves:** 2

Ingredients:

- 2 pounds Brussels sprouts
- 2 tablespoons avocado oil
- Salt and pepper, to taste
- 1 cup pine nuts, roasted

Directions:

1. Trim the bottom of the Brussels sprouts.
2. Take a bowl and combine the avocado oil, salt, and black pepper.
3. Toss the Brussels sprouts into the bowl and mix well.
4. Divide the mixture into both air fryer baskets.
5. For zone 1 set to AIR FRY mode for 20 minutes at 390 degrees F.
6. Select the MATCH button for the zone 2 basket.

7. Once the Brussels sprouts get crisp and tender, take out and serve.

Serving Suggestion: Serve with rice.

Variation Tip: Use olive oil instead of avocado oil.

Per Serving: Calories 672; Fat 50g; Sodium 115mg; Carbs 51g; Fiber 20.2g; Sugar 12.3g; Protein 25g

Lime Glazed Tofu

Prep time: 10 minutes| **Cook time:** 14 minutes| **Serves:** 6

Ingredients:

- ⅔ cup coconut aminos
- 2 (14-oz) packages extra-firm, water-packed tofu, drained
- 6 tablespoons toasted sesame oil
- ⅔ cup lime juice

Directions:

1. Pat dry the tofu bars and slice into half-inch cubes.
2. Toss all the remaining Ingredients: in a small bowl.
3. Marinate for 4 hours in the refrigerator. Drain off the excess water.
4. Divide the tofu cubes in the two crisper plates.
5. Return the crisper plates to the Ninja Foodi 2-Basket Air Fryer.
6. Choose the Air Fry mode for Zone 1 and set the temperature to 400 degrees F and the time to 14 minutes.
7. Select the "MATCH" button to copy the settings for Zone 2.
8. Initiate cooking by pressing the START/STOP button.
9. Toss the tofu once cooked halfway through, then resume cooking.
10. Serve warm.

Serving Suggestion: Serve with sautéed green vegetables.

Variation Tip: Add sautéed onion and carrot to the tofu cubes.

Per Serving: Calories 284; Fat 7.9g; Sodium 704mg; Carbs 38.1g; Fiber 1.9g; Sugar 1.9g; Protein 14.8g

Kale and Spinach Chips

Prep time: 12 minutes| **Cook time:** 6 minutes| **Serves:** 2

Ingredients:

- 2 cups spinach, torn in pieces and stem removed
- 2 cups kale, torn in pieces, stems removed
- 1 tablespoon olive oil
- Sea salt, to taste
- ⅓ cup Parmesan cheese

Directions:

1. Take a bowl and add spinach to it.

2. Take another bowl and add kale to it.
3. Season both of them with olive oil and sea salt.
4. Add the kale to the zone 1 basket and spinach to the zone 2 basket.
5. Select AIR FRY mode for zone 1 at 350 degrees F for 6 minutes.
6. Set zone 2 to AIR FRY mode at 350 degrees F for 5 minutes.
7. Once done, take out the crispy chips and sprinkle Parmesan cheese on top.
8. Serve and Enjoy.

Serving Suggestion: Serve with baked potato.

Variation Tip: Use canola oil instead of olive oil.

Per Serving: Calories 166; Fat 11.1g; Sodium 355mg; Carbs 8.1g; Fiber 1.7 g; Sugar 0.1g; Protein 8.2g

Zucchini with Stuffing

Prep time: 12 minutes| **Cook time:** 20 minutes| **Serves:** 3

Ingredients:

- 1 cup quinoa, rinsed
- 1 cup black olives
- 6 medium zucchinis, about 2 pounds
- 2 cups cannellini beans, drained
- 1 white onion, chopped
- ¼ cup almonds, chopped
- 4 cloves garlic, chopped
- 4 tablespoons olive oil
- 1 cup water
- 2 cups Parmesan cheese, for topping

Directions:

1. First wash the zucchini and cut it lengthwise.
2. Take a skillet and heat oil in it
3. Sauté the onion in olive oil for a few minutes.
4. Then add the quinoa and water and let it cook for 8 minutes with the lid on top.
5. Transfer the quinoa to a bowl and add all the remaining Ingredients, excluding zucchini and Parmesan cheese.
6. Scoop out the seeds of the zucchinis.
7. Fill the cavity of zucchinis with the quinoa mixture.
8. Top it with a handful of Parmesan cheese.
9. Arrange the zucchinis in both air fryer baskets.
10. Select zone 1 basket at AIR FRY mode for 20 minutes and temperature to 390 degrees F.
11. Use the MATCH button to select the same setting for zone 2.
12. Serve and enjoy.

Serving Suggestion: Serve them with pasta.

Variation Tip: None.

Per Serving: Calories 1171; Fat 48.6g; Sodium 1747mg; Carbs 132.4g; Fiber 42.1g; Sugar 11.5g; Protein 65.7g

Cheesy Potatoes with Asparagus

Prep time: 15 minutes| **Cook time:** 35 minutes| **Serves:** 2

Ingredients:

- 1½ pounds russet potato, wedges or cut in half
- 2 teaspoons mixed herbs
- 2 teaspoons chili flakes
- 2 cups asparagus
- 1 cup chopped onion
- 1 tablespoon Dijon mustard
- ¼ cup fresh cream
- 1 teaspoon olive oil
- 2 tablespoons butter
- ½ teaspoon salt and black pepper
- Water as required
- ½ cup Parmesan cheese

Directions:

1. Take a bowl and add asparagus and sweet potato wedges to it.
2. Season it with salt, black pepper, and olive oil.
3. Add the potato wedges to the zone 1 air fryer basket and asparagus to the zone 2 basket.
4. Set zone 1 to AIR FRY mode at 390 degrees F for 12 minutes.
5. Set the zone 2 basket to AIR FRY mode at 390 degrees F for 30-35 minutes. Click Sync button.
6. Meanwhile, take a skillet and add butter and sauté the onion in it for a few minutes.
7. Then add salt and Dijon mustard and chili flakes, Parmesan cheese, and fresh cream.
8. Once the veggies are cooked take them out and drizzle the cream mixture on top.

Serving Suggestion: Serve with rice.

Variation Tip: Use olive oil instead of butter.

Per Serving: Calories 251; Fat 11g; Sodium 279mg; Carbs 31.1g; Fiber 5g; Sugar 4.1g; Protein 9g

Stuffed Tomatoes

Prep time: 12 minutes| **Cook time:** 8 minutes| **Serves:** 2

Ingredients:

- 2 cups brown rice, cooked
- 1 cup tofu, grilled and chopped
- 4 large red tomatoes
- 4 tablespoons basil, chopped
- ¼ tablespoon olive oil
- Salt and black pepper, to taste
- 2 tablespoons lemon juice
- 1 teaspoon red chili powder
- ½ cup Parmesan cheese

Directions:

1. Take a large bowl and mix rice, tofu, basil, olive oil, salt, black pepper, lemon juice, and chili powder.
2. Core the center of the tomatoes.
3. Fill the cavity with the rice mixture.
4. Top them off with the cheese sprinkle.
5. Divide the tomatoes into two air fryer baskets.
6. Turn zone 1 to AIR FRY mode for 8 minutes at 400 degrees F.
7. Select the MATCH button for zone 2.
8. Serve and enjoy.

Serving Suggestion: Serve it with Greek yogurt.

Variation Tip: Use canola oil instead of olive oil.

Per Serving: Calories 1034; Fat 24.2g; Sodium 527mg; Carbs 165g; Fiber 12.1g; Sugar 1.2g; Protein 43.9g

Quinoa Patties

Prep time: 15 minutes| **Cook time:** 32 minutes| **Serves:** 4

Ingredients:

- 1 cup quinoa red
- 1½ cups water
- 1 teaspoon salt
- black pepper, ground
- 1½ cups rolled oats
- 3 eggs beaten
- ¼ cup minced white onion
- ½ cup crumbled feta cheese
- ¼ cup chopped fresh chives
- Salt and black pepper, to taste
- Vegetable or canola oil
- 4 hamburger buns
- 4 arugulas
- 4 slices tomato sliced

Cucumber yogurt dill sauce

- 1 cup cucumber, diced
- 1 cup Greek yogurt
- 2 teaspoons lemon juice
- ¼ teaspoon salt
- Black pepper, ground
- 1 tablespoon chopped fresh dill
- 1 tablespoon olive oil

Directions:

1. Add quinoa to a saucepan filled with cold water, salt, and black pepper, and place it over medium-high heat.
2. Cook the quinoa to a boil, then reduce the heat, cover, and cook for 20 minutes on a simmer.
3. Fluff and mix the cooked quinoa with a fork and remove it from the heat.

4. Spread the quinoa in a baking stay.
5. Mix eggs, oats, onion, herbs, cheese, salt, and black pepper.
6. Stir in quinoa, then mix well. Make 4 patties out of this quinoa cheese mixture.
7. Divide the patties in the two crisper plates and spray them with cooking oil.
8. Return the crisper plates to the Ninja Foodi 2-Basket Air Fryer.
9. Choose the Air Fry mode for Zone 1 and set the temperature to 390 degrees F and the time to 13 minutes.
10. Select the "MATCH" button to copy the settings for Zone 2.
11. Initiate cooking by pressing the START/STOP button.
12. Flip the patties once cooked halfway through, and resume cooking.
13. Meanwhile, prepare the cucumber yogurt dill sauce by mixing all of its Ingredients: in a mixing bowl.
14. Place each quinoa patty in a burger bun along with arugula leaves.
15. Serve with yogurt dill sauce.

Serving Suggestion: Serve with yogurt dip.

Variation Tip: Use crushed cornflakes for breading to have extra crispiness.

Per Serving: Calories 231; Fat 9g; Sodium 271mg; Carbs 32.8g; Fiber 6.4g; Sugar 7g; Protein 6.3g

Curly Fries

Prep time: 10 minutes| **Cook time:** 20 minutes| **Serves:** 6

Ingredients:

- 2 spiralized zucchinis
- 1 cup flour
- 2 tablespoons paprika
- 1 teaspoon cayenne pepper
- 1 teaspoon garlic powder
- 1 teaspoon black pepper
- 1 teaspoon salt
- 2 eggs
- Olive oil or cooking spray

Directions:

1. Mix flour with paprika, cayenne pepper, garlic powder, black pepper, and salt in a bowl.
2. Beat eggs in another bowl and dip the zucchini in the eggs.
3. Coat the zucchini with the flour mixture and divide it into two crisper plates.
4. Spray the zucchini with cooking oil.
5. Return the crisper plate to the Ninja Foodi 2-Basket Air Fryer.
6. Choose the Air Fry mode for Zone 1 and set the temperature to 400 degrees F and the time to 20 minutes.
7. Select the "MATCH" button to copy the settings for Zone 2.
8. Initiate cooking by pressing the START/STOP button.
9. Toss the zucchini once cooked halfway through, then resume cooking.
10. Serve warm.

Serving Suggestion: Serve with red chunky salsa or chili sauce.

Variation Tip: Use crushed cornflakes for breading to have extra crispiness.

Per Serving: Calories 212; Fat 11.8g; Sodium 321mg; Carbs 24.6g; Fiber 4.4g; Sugar 8g; Protein 7.3g

Fried Artichoke Hearts

Prep time: 15 minutes| **Cook time:** 10 minutes| **Serves:** 6

Ingredients:

- 3 cans quartered artichokes, drained
- ½ cup mayonnaise
- 1 cup panko breadcrumbs
- ⅓ cup grated Parmesan
- salt and black pepper to taste
- Parsley for garnish

Directions:

1. Mix mayonnaise with salt and black pepper and keep the sauce aside.
2. Spread panko breadcrumbs in a bowl.
3. Coat the artichoke pieces with the breadcrumbs.
4. As you coat the artichokes, place them in the two crisper plates in a single layer, then spray them with cooking oil.
5. Return the crisper plates to the Ninja Foodi 2-Basket Air Fryer.
6. Choose the Air Fry mode for Zone 1 and set the temperature to 375 degrees F and the time to 10 minutes.
7. Select the "MATCH" button to copy the settings for Zone 2.
8. Initiate cooking by pressing the START/STOP button.
9. Flip the artichokes once cooked halfway through, then resume cooking.
10. Serve warm with mayo sauce.

Serving Suggestion: Serve with red chunky salsa or chili sauce.

Variation Tip: Use crushed cornflakes for breading to have extra crispiness.

Per Serving: Calories 193; Fat 1g; Sodium 395mg; Carbs 38.7g; Fiber 1.6g; Sugar 0.9g; Protein 6.6g

Falafel

Prep time: 15 minutes| **Cook time:** 14 minutes| **Serves:** 6

Ingredients:

- 1 (15.5-oz) can chickpeas, rinsed and drained
- 1 small yellow onion, cut into quarters
- 3 garlic cloves, chopped
- ⅓ cup parsley, chopped
- ⅓ cup cilantro, chopped
- ⅓ cup scallions, chopped
- 1 teaspoon cumin
- ½ teaspoons salt
- ⅛ teaspoons crushed red pepper flakes
- 1 teaspoon baking powder
- 4 tablespoons all-purpose flour
- Olive oil spray

Directions:

1. Dry the chickpeas on paper towels.
2. Add onions and garlic to a food processor and chop them.
3. Add the parsley, salt, cilantro, scallions, cumin, and red pepper flakes.
4. Press the START/STOP button for 60 seconds, then toss in chickpeas and blend for 3 times until it makes a chunky paste.
5. Stir in baking powder and flour and mix well.
6. Transfer the falafel mixture to a bowl and cover to refrigerate for 3 hours.
7. Make 12 balls out of the falafel mixture.
8. Place 6 falafels in each of the crisper plate and spray them with oil.
9. Return the crisper plate to the Ninja Foodi 2-Basket Air Fryer.
10. Choose the Air Fry mode for Zone 1 and set the temperature to 350 degrees F and the time to 14 minutes.
11. Select the "MATCH" button to copy the settings for Zone 2.
12. Initiate cooking by pressing the START/STOP button.
13. Toss the falafel once cooked halfway through, and resume cooking.
14. Serve warm.

Serving Suggestion: Serve with yogurt dip and sautéed carrots.

Variation Tip: Use breadcrumbs for breading to have extra crispiness.

Per Serving: Calories 113; Fat 3g; Sodium 152mg; Carbs 20g; Fiber 3g; Sugar 1.1g; Protein 3.5g

Air Fried Okra

Prep time: 10 minutes| **Cook time:** 13 minutes| **Serves:** 2

Ingredients:

- ½ lb. okra pods sliced
- 1 teaspoon olive oil
- ¼ teaspoon salt
- ⅛ teaspoon black pepper

Directions:

1. Preheat the Ninja Foodi 2-Basket Air Fryer to 350 degrees F.
2. Toss okra with olive oil, salt, and black pepper in a bowl.
3. Spread the okra in a single layer in the two crisper plates.
4. Return the crisper plate to the Ninja Foodi 2-Basket Air Fryer.
5. Choose the Air Fry mode for Zone 1 and set the temperature to 375 degrees F and the time to 13 minutes.
6. Select the "MATCH" button to copy the settings for Zone 2.
7. Initiate cooking by pressing the START/STOP button.
8. Toss the okra once cooked halfway through, and resume cooking.
9. Serve warm.

Serving Suggestion: Serve with potato chips and bread slices.

Variation Tip: Sprinkle cornmeal before cooking for added crisp.

Per Serving: Calories 208; Fat 5g; Sodium 1205mg; Carbs 34.1g; Fiber 7.8g; Sugar 2.5g; Protein 5.9g

Fried Olives

Prep time: 15 minutes| **Cook time:** 9 minutes| **Serves:** 6

Ingredients:

- 2 cups blue cheese stuffed olives, drained
- ½ cup all-purpose flour
- 1 cup panko breadcrumbs
- ½ teaspoon garlic powder
- 1 pinch oregano
- 2 eggs

Directions:

1. Mix flour with oregano and garlic powder in a bowl and beat two eggs in another bowl.
2. Spread panko breadcrumbs in a bowl.
3. Coat all the olives with the flour mixture, dip in the eggs and then coat with the panko breadcrumbs.
4. As you coat the olives, place them in the two crisper plates in a single layer, then spray them with cooking oil.
5. Return the crisper plates to the Ninja Foodi 2-Basket Air Fryer.
6. Choose the Air Fry mode for Zone 1 and set the temperature to 375 degrees F and the time to 9 minutes.
7. Select the "MATCH" button to copy the settings for Zone 2.
8. Initiate cooking by pressing the START/STOP button.
9. Flip the olives once cooked halfway through, then resume cooking.
10. Serve.

Serving Suggestion: Serve with red chunky salsa or chili sauce.

Variation Tip: Use crushed cornflakes for breading to have extra crispiness.

Per Serving: Calories 166; Fat 3.2g; Sodium 437mg; Carbs 28.8g; Fiber 1.8g; Sugar 2.7g; Protein 5.8g

Fish and Seafood Recipes

Two-Way Salmon

Prep time: 10 minutes| **Cook time:** 18 minutes| **Serves:** 2

Ingredients:

- 2 salmon fillets, 8 ounces each
- 2 tablespoons Cajun seasoning
- 2 tablespoons Jerk seasoning
- 1 lemon cut in half
- Oil spray, for greasing

Directions:

1. First, drizzle lemon juice over the salmon and wash them with tap water.
2. Rinse and pat dry the fillets with a paper towel.
3. Rub the fillets with Cajun seasoning and grease with oil spray.
4. Take the second fillet and rub it with Jerk seasoning.
5. Grease the second fillet of with oil spray.
6. Place the salmon fillets in both the baskets.
7. Set the zone 1 basket to 390 degrees F for 16-18 minutes.
8. Select MATCH button for zone 2 basket.
9. Hit the START/STOP button to start cooking.
10. Once the cooking is done, serve the fish hot with mayonnaise.

Serving Suggestion: Serve it with ranch.

Variation Tip: None.

Per Serving: Calories 238; Fat 11.8g; Sodium 488mg; Carbs 9g; Fiber 0g; Sugar 8g; Protein 35g

Salmon with Green Beans

Prep time: 12 minutes| **Cook time:** 18 minutes| **Serves:** 1

Ingredients:

- 1 salmon fillet, 2-inch-thick
- 2 teaspoons olive oil
- 2 teaspoons smoked Paprika
- Salt and black pepper, to taste
- 1 cup green beans
- Oil spray, for greasing

Directions:

1. Grease the green beans with oil spray and add them to the zone 1 basket.
2. Rub the salmon fillet with olive oil, smoked Paprika, salt, and black pepper.
3. Put the salmon fillet in the zone 2 basket.

4. Set the zone 1 basket to AIR FRY mode at 350 degrees F for 18 minutes.
5. Set the zone 2 basket to 390 degrees F for 16-18 minutes.
6. Hit the Sync button so that they both finish at the same time.
7. Once done, take out the salmon and green beans, transfer them to the serving plates and enjoy.

Serving Suggestion: Serve it with ranch.

Variation Tip: Use any other green vegetable of your choice.

Per Serving: Calories 367; Fat 22 g; Sodium 87mg; Carbs 10.2g; Fiber 5.3g; Sugar 2g; Protein 37.2g

Fish Sandwich

Prep time: 15 minutes| **Cook time:** 22 minutes| **Serves:** 4

Ingredients:

- 4 small cod fillets, skinless
- Salt and black pepper, to taste
- 2 tablespoons flour
- ¼ cup dried breadcrumbs
- Spray oil
- 9 ounces of frozen peas
- 1 tablespoon creme fraiche
- 12 capers
- 1 squeeze of lemon juice
- 4 bread rolls, cut in halve

Directions:

1. First, coat the cod fillets with flour, salt, and black pepper.
2. Then coat the fish with breadcrumbs.
3. Divide the coated codfish in the two crisper plates and spray them with cooking spray.
4. Return the crisper plate to the Ninja Foodi 2-Basket Air Fryer.
5. Choose the Air Fry mode for Zone 1 and set the temperature to 390 degrees F and the time to 17 minutes.
6. Select the "MATCH" button to copy the settings for Zone 2.
7. Initiate cooking by pressing the START/STOP button.
8. Meanwhile, boil peas in hot water for 5 minutes until soft.
9. Then drain the peas and transfer them to the blender.
10. Add capers, lemon juice, and crème fraiche to the blender.
11. Blend until it makes a smooth mixture.
12. Spread the peas crème mixture on top of 2 lower halves of the bread roll, and place the fish fillets on it.
13. Place the remaining bread slices on top.
14. Serve fresh.

Serving Suggestion: Serve with sautéed or fresh greens with melted butter.

Variation Tip: Coat the fish with crushed cornflakes for extra crispiness.

Per Serving: Calories 348; Fat 30g; Sodium 660mg; Carbs 5g; Fiber 0g; Sugar 0g; Protein 14g

Codfish with Herb Vinaigrette

Prep time: 15 minutes| **Cook time:** 16 minutes| **Serves:** 2

Ingredients:

Vinaigrette Ingredients:

- ½ cup parsley leaves
- 1 cup basil leaves
- ½ cup mint leaves
- 2 tablespoons thyme leaves
- ¼ teaspoon red pepper flakes
- 2 cloves garlic
- 4 tablespoons red wine vinegar
- ¼ cup olive oil
- Salt, to taste

Other Ingredients:

- 1.5 pounds fish fillets, codfish
- 2 tablespoons olive oil
- Salt and black pepper, to taste
- 1 teaspoon Paprika
- 1 teaspoon Italian seasoning

Directions:

1. Blend the entire vinaigrette Ingredients: in a high-speed blender and pulse into a smooth paste.
2. Set aside for drizzling over the cooked fish.
3. Rub the fillets with salt, black pepper, paprika, Italian seasoning, and olive oil.
4. Divide the between two baskets of the air fryer.
5. Set zone 1 to 16 minutes at 390 degrees F, on AIR FRY mode.
6. Press the MATCH button for zone 2.
7. Once done, serve the fillets with a drizzle of blended vinaigrette on top.

Serving Suggestion: Serve it with rice.

Variation Tip: Use sour cream instead of cream cheese.

Per Serving: Calories 1219; Fat 81.8g; Sodium 1906mg; Carbs 64.4g; Fiber 5.5g; Sugar 0.4g; Protein 52.1g

Buttered Mahi-Mahi

Prep time: 15 minutes| **Cook time:** 22 minutes| **Serves:** 4

Ingredients:

- 4 (6-oz) mahi-mahi fillets
- Salt and black pepper ground to taste
- Cooking spray
- ⅔ cup butter

Directions:

1. Preheat your Ninja Foodi 2-Basket Air Fryer to 350 degrees F.
2. Rub the mahi-mahi fillets with salt and black pepper.
3. Place two mahi-mahi fillets in each of the crisper plate.

4. Return the crisper plates to the Ninja Foodi 2-Basket Air Fryer.
5. Choose the Air Fry mode for Zone 1 and set the temperature to 390 degrees F and the time to 17 minutes.
6. Select the "MATCH" button to copy the settings for Zone 2.
7. Initiate cooking by pressing the START/STOP button.
8. Add butter to a saucepan and cook for 5 minutes until slightly brown.
9. Remove the butter from the heat.
10. Drizzle butter over the fish and serve warm.

Serving Suggestion: Serve with pasta or fried rice.

Variation Tip: Drizzle parmesan cheese on top.

Per Serving: Calories 399; Fat 16g; Sodium 537mg; Carbs 28g; Fiber 3g; Sugar 10g; Protein 35g

Beer Battered Fish Fillet

Prep time: 18 minutes| **Cook time:** 14 minutes| **Serves:** 2

Ingredients:

- 1 cup all-purpose flour
- 4 tablespoons cornstarch
- 1 teaspoon baking soda
- 8 ounces beer
- 2 egg beaten
- 1 teaspoon smoked Paprika
- 1 teaspoon salt
- ¼ teaspoon freshly ground black pepper
- ¼ teaspoon cayenne pepper
- 2 cod fillets, 1½-inches thick, cut into 4 pieces
- Oil spray, for greasing

Directions:

1. Take a large bowl and combine 1 cup flour, baking soda, cornstarch, and salt.
2. In a separate bowl, beat the eggs along with the beer.
3. In a shallow dish, mix paprika, salt, pepper, and cayenne pepper.
4. Dry the codfish fillets with a paper towel.
5. Dip the fish into the eggs and coat them with the flour mixture.
6. Then dip it in the seasoning.
7. Grease the fillets with oil spray.
8. Divide the fillets between both zones.
9. Set zone 1 to AIR FRY mode at 400 degrees F for 14 minutes.
10. Select MATCH button for zone 2 basket.
11. Press START/STOP button and let them cook.
12. Once the cooking is done, serve the fish.
13. Enjoy it hot.

Serving Suggestion: Serve it with rice.

Variation Tip: Use mild Paprika instead of smoked Paprika.

Per Serving: Calories 1691; Fat 6.1g; Sodium 3976mg; Carbs 105.1 g; Fiber 3.4g; Sugar 15.6 g; Protein 270g

Salmon with Broccoli and Cheese

Prep time: 15 minutes| **Cook time:** 18 minutes| **Serves:** 2

Ingredients:

- 2 cups broccoli
- ½ cup butter, melted
- Salt and pepper, to taste
- Oil spray, for greasing
- 1 cup grated Cheddar cheese
- 1 pound salmon, fillets

Directions:

1. Take a bowl and add broccoli to it.
2. Add salt and black pepper and spray the broccoli with oil.
3. Put the broccoli in the air fryer zone 1 basket.
4. Rub the salmon fillets with salt, black pepper, and butter.
5. Place them into zone 2 basket.
6. Set zone 1 to AIR FRY mode for 5 minters at 400 degrees F.
7. Set zone 2 to AIR FRY mode for 18 minutes at 390 degrees F.
8. Sprinkle the grated cheese on top of the salmon and serve.

Serving Suggestion: Serve with rice and baked potato.

Variation Tip: Use olive oil instead of butter.

Per Serving: Calories 966; Fat 79.1g; Sodium 808mg; Carbs 6.8g; Fiber 2.4g; Sugar 1.9g; Protein 61.2g

Salmon with Coconut

Prep time: 10 minutes| **Cook time:** 15 minutes| **Serves:** 2

Ingredients:

- Oil spray, for greasing
- 2 salmon fillets, 6 ounces each
- Salt and ground black pepper, to taste
- 1 tablespoon butter, for frying
- 1 tablespoon red curry paste
- 1 cup coconut cream
- 2 tablespoons fresh cilantro, chopped
- 1 cup cauliflower florets
- ½ cup Parmesan cheese, hard

Directions:

1. Mix salt, black pepper, butter, red curry paste, coconut cream in a bowl and marinate the salmon in it.
2. Oil spray the cauliflower florets and then season with salt and freshly ground black pepper.
3. Place the florets in the zone 1 basket.
4. Layer parchment paper over the zone 2 basket, and then place the salmon fillets on it.

5. Set the zone 2 basket to AIR FRY mode at 15 minutes for 400 degrees F
6. Hit the Sync button to finish it at the same time.
7. Once the time for cooking is over, serve the salmon with cauliflower florets with Parmesan cheese sprinkled on top.

Serving Suggestion: Serve with rice.

Variation Tip: Use Mozzarella cheese instead of Parmesan cheese.

Per Serving: Calories 774; Fat 59g; Sodium 1223mg; Carbs 12.2g; Fiber 3.9g; Sugar 5.9g; Protein 53.5g

Smoked Salmon

Prep time: 20 minutes| **Cook time:** 12 minutes| **Serves:** 4

Ingredients:

- 2 pounds salmon fillets, smoked
- 6 ounces cream cheese
- 4 tablespoons mayonnaise
- 2 teaspoons chives, fresh
- 1 teaspoon lemon zest
- Salt and freshly ground black pepper, to taste
- 2 tablespoons butter

Directions:

1. Cut the salmon into very small and uniform bite-size pieces.
2. Mix cream cheese, chives, mayonnaise, black pepper, and lemon zest, in a small mixing bowl.
3. Set it aside for further use.
4. Coat the salmon pieces with salt and butter.
5. Divide the bite-size pieces into both zones of the air fryer.
6. Set it on AIR FRY mode at 400 degrees F for 12 minutes.
7. Select MATCH for zone 2 basket.
8. Once the salmon is done, top it with the cream cheese mixture and serve.
9. Enjoy hot.

Serving Suggestion: Serve it with rice.

Variation Tip: Use sour cream instead of cream cheese.

Per Serving: Calories 557; Fat 15.7g; Sodium 371mg; Carbs 4.8g; Fiber 0g; Sugar 1.1g; Protein 48g

Salmon with Fennel Salad

Prep time: 10 minutes| **Cook time:** 17 minutes| **Serves:** 4

Ingredients:

- 2 teaspoons fresh parsley, chopped
- 1 teaspoon fresh thyme, chopped
- 1 teaspoon salt
- 4 (6-oz) skinless center-cut salmon fillets
- 2 tablespoons olive oil
- 4 cups fennel, sliced
- ⅔ cup Greek yogurt
- 1 garlic clove, grated

- 2 tablespoons orange juice
- 1 teaspoon lemon juice
- 2 tablespoons fresh dill, chopped

Directions:

1. Preheat your Ninja Foodi 2-Basket Air Fryer to 200 degrees F.
2. Mix ½ teaspoon of salt, thyme, and parsley in a small bowl.
3. Brush the salmon with oil first, then rub liberally rub the herb mixture.
4. Place 2 salmon fillets in each of the crisper plate.
5. Return the crisper plate to the Ninja Foodi 2-Basket Air Fryer.
6. Choose the Air Fry mode for Zone 1 and set the temperature to 390 degrees F and the time to 17 minutes.
7. Select the "MATCH" button to copy the settings for Zone 2.
8. Initiate cooking by pressing the START/STOP button.
9. Meanwhile, mix fennel with garlic, yogurt, lemon juice, orange juice, remaining salt, and dill in a mixing bowl.
10. Serve the air fried salmon fillets with fennel salad.
11. Enjoy.

Serving Suggestion: Serve with melted butter on top.

Variation Tip: Rub the salmon with lemon juice before cooking.

Per Serving: Calories 305; Fat 15g; Sodium 482mg; Carbs 17g; Fiber 3g; Sugar 2g; Protein 35g

Seafood Shrimp Omelet

Prep time: 20 minutes | **Cook time:** 15 minutes | **Serves:** 2

Ingredients:

- 6 large shrimp, shells removed and chopped
- 6 eggs, beaten
- ½ tablespoon butter, melted
- 2 tablespoons green onions, sliced
- ⅓ cup mushrooms, chopped
- 1 pinch Paprika
- Salt and black pepper, to taste
- Oil spray, for greasing

Directions:

1. In a large bowl, whisk the eggs and add the chopped shrimp, butter, green onions, mushrooms, paprika, salt, and black pepper.
2. Take two cake pans that fit inside the air fryer and grease them with oil spray.
3. Pour the egg mixture between the cake pans and place it in the air fryer baskets.
4. Set zone 1 to BAKE mode and set the temperature to 320 degrees F for 15 minutes.
5. Select the MATCH button to match the cooking time for the zone 2 basket.
6. Once the cooking cycle is complete, take out, and serve hot.

Serving Suggestion: Serve it with rice.

Variation Tip: Use olive oil for greasing purposes.

Per Serving: Calories 300; Fat 17.5g; Sodium 368mg; Carbs 2.9g; Fiber 0.3g; Sugar 1.4 g; Protein 32.2g

Crusted Tilapia

Prep time: 20 minutes| **Cook time:** 17 minutes| **Serves:** 4

Ingredients:

- ¾ cup breadcrumbs
- 1 packet dry ranch-style dressing
- 2½ tablespoons vegetable oil
- 2 eggs beaten
- 4 tilapia fillets
- Herbs and chilies to garnish

Directions:

1. Thoroughly mix ranch dressing with panko in a bowl.
2. Whisk eggs in a shallow bowl.
3. Dip each fish fillet in the egg, then coat evenly with the panko mixture.
4. Set two coated fillets in each of the crisper plate.
5. Return the crisper plates to the Ninja Foodi 2-Basket Air Fryer.
6. Choose the Air Fry mode for Zone 1 and set the temperature to 390 degrees F and the time to 17 minutes.
7. Select the "MATCH" button to copy the settings for Zone 2.
8. Initiate cooking by pressing the START/STOP button.
9. Serve warm with herbs and chilies.

Serving Suggestion: Serve with sautéed asparagus on the side.

Variation Tip: Coat the fish with crushed cornflakes for extra crispiness.

Per Serving: Calories 196; Fat 7.1g; Sodium 492mg; Carbs 21.6g; Fiber 2.9g; Sugar 0.8g; Protein 13.4g

Salmon Nuggets

Prep time: 15 minutes| **Cook time:** 15 minutes| **Serves:** 4

Ingredients:

- ⅓ cup maple syrup
- ¼ teaspoon dried chipotle pepper
- 1 pinch sea salt
- 1 ½ cups croutons
- 1 large egg
- 1 (1 pound) skinless salmon fillet, cut into 1 ½-inch chunk
- cooking spray

Directions:

1. Mix chipotle powder, maple syrup, and salt in a saucepan and cook on a simmer for 5 minutes.
2. Crush the croutons in a food processor and transfer to a bowl.
3. Beat egg in another shallow bowl.
4. Season the salmon chunks with sea salt.
5. Dip the salmon in the egg, then coat with breadcrumbs.

6. Divide the coated salmon chunks in the two crisper plates.
7. Return the crisper plate to the Ninja Foodi 2-Basket Air Fryer.
8. Select the Air Fry mode for Zone 1 and set the temperature to 390 degrees F and the time to 10 minutes.
9. Press the "MATCH" button to copy the settings for Zone 2.
10. Initiate cooking by pressing the START/STOP button.
11. Flip the chunks once cooked halfway through, then resume cooking.
12. Pour the maple syrup on top and serve warm.

Serving Suggestion: Serve with creamy dip and crispy fries.

Variation Tip: Use crushed cornflakes for breading to have extra crispiness.

Per Serving: Calories 275; Fat 1.4g; Sodium 582mg; Carbs 31.5g; Fiber 1.1g; Sugar 0.1g; Protein 29.8g

Savory Salmon Fillets

Prep time: 10 minutes| **Cook time:** 17 minutes| **Serves:** 4

Ingredients:

- 4 (6-oz) salmon fillets
- Salt, to taste
- Black pepper, to taste
- 4 teaspoons olive oil
- 4 tablespoons wholegrain mustard
- 2 tablespoons packed brown sugar
- 2 garlic cloves, minced
- 1 teaspoon thyme leaves

Directions:

1. Rub the salmon with salt and black pepper first.
2. Whisk oil with sugar, thyme, garlic, and mustard in a small bowl.
3. Place two salmon fillets in each of the crisper plate and brush the thyme mixture on top of each fillet.
4. Return the crisper plates to the Ninja Foodi 2-Basket Air Fryer.
5. Choose the Air Fry mode for Zone 1 and set the temperature to 390 degrees F and the time to 17 minutes.
6. Select the "MATCH" button to copy the settings for Zone 2.
7. Initiate cooking by pressing the START/STOP button.
8. Serve warm and fresh.

Serving Suggestion: Serve with parsley and melted butter on top.

Variation Tip: Rub the fish fillets with lemon juice before cooking.

Per Serving: Calories 336; Fat 6g; Sodium 181mg; Carbs 1.3g; Fiber 0.2g; Sugar 0.4g; Protein 69.2g

Fried Lobster Tails

Prep time: 10 minutes| **Cook time:** 18 minutes| **Serves:** 4

Ingredients:

- 4 (4-oz) lobster tails
- 8 tablespoons butter, melted
- 2 teaspoons lemon zest
- 2 garlic cloves, grated
- Salt and black pepper, ground to taste
- 2 teaspoons fresh parsley, chopped
- 4 wedges lemon

Directions:

1. Spread the lobster tails into Butterfly, slit the top to expose the lobster meat while keeping the tail intact.
2. Place two lobster tails in each of the crisper plate with their lobster meat facing up.
3. Mix melted butter with lemon zest and garlic in a bowl.
4. Brush the butter mixture on top of the lobster tails.
5. And drizzle salt and black pepper on top.
6. Return the crisper plate to the Ninja Foodi 2-Basket Air Fryer.
7. Choose the Air Fry mode for Zone 1 and set the temperature to 390 degrees F and the time to 18 minutes.
8. Select the "MATCH" button to copy the settings for Zone 2.
9. Initiate cooking by pressing the START/STOP button.
10. Garnish with parsley and lemon wedges.
11. Serve warm.

Serving Suggestion: Serve on a bed of lettuce leaves.

Variation Tip: Drizzle crushed cornflakes on top to have extra crispiness.

Per Serving: Calories 257; Fat 10.4g; Sodium 431mg; Carbs 20g; Fiber 0g; Sugar 1.6g; Protein 21g

Crusted Shrimp

Prep time: 20 minutes| **Cook time:** 13 minutes| **Serves:** 4

Ingredients:

- 1 lb. shrimp
- ½ cup flour, all-purpose
- 1 teaspoon salt
- ½ teaspoon baking powder
- ⅔ cup water
- 2 cups coconut shred
- ½ cup bread crumbs

Directions:

1. In a small bowl, whisk together flour, salt, water, and baking powder. Set aside for 5 minutes.
2. In another shallow bowl, toss bread crumbs with coconut shreds together.
3. Dredge shrimp in liquid, then coat in coconut mixture, making sure it's totally covered.

4. Repeat until all shrimp are coated.
5. Spread half of the shrimp in each crisper plate and spray them with cooking oil.
6. Return the crisper plates to the Ninja Foodi 2-Basket Air Fryer.
7. Choose the Air Fry mode for Zone 1 and set the temperature to 390 degrees F and the time to 13 minutes.
8. Select the "MATCH" button to copy the settings for Zone 2.
9. Initiate cooking by pressing the START/STOP button.
10. Shake the baskets once cooked halfway, then resume cooking.
11. Serve with your favorite dip.

Serving Suggestion: Serve on top of mashed potato or mashed cauliflower.

Variation Tip: Use crushed cornflakes for breading to have extra crispiness.

Per Serving: Calories 297; Fat 1g; Sodium 291mg; Carbs 35g; Fiber 1g; Sugar 9g; Protein 29g

Poultry Mains Recipes

Cornish Hen with Baked Potatoes

Prep time: 20 minutes| **Cook time:** 45 minutes| **Serves:** 2

Ingredients:

- Salt, to taste
- 1 large potato
- 1 tablespoon avocado oil
- 1.5 pounds Cornish hen, skinless and whole
- 2-3 teaspoons poultry seasoning, dry rub

Directions:

1. Pierce the large potato with a fork.
2. Rub the potato with avocado oil and salt.
3. Place the potato in the first basket.
4. Coat the Cornish hen thoroughly with poultry seasoning (dry rub) and salt.
5. Place the hen in zone 2 basket.
6. Set zone 1 to AIR FRY mode at 350 degrees F for 45 minutes.
7. For zone 2 press the MATCH button.
8. Once the cooking cycle is complete, turn off the air fryer and take out the potatoes and Cornish hen from both air fryer baskets.
9. Serve hot and enjoy.

Serving Suggestion: Serve it with coleslaw.

Variation Tip: You can use olive oil or canola oil instead of avocado oil.

Per Serving: Calories 612; Fat 14.3g; Sodium 304mg; Carbs 33.4 g; Fiber 4.5g; Sugar 1.5g; Protein 83.2g

Chicken & Broccoli

Prep time: 22 minutes| **Cook time:** 35 minutes| **Serves:** 2

Ingredients:

- 1 pound chicken, boneless & bite-size pieces
- 1½ cups broccoli
- 2 tablespoons grapeseed oil
- ⅓ teaspoon garlic powder
- 1 teaspoon ginger and garlic paste
- 2 teaspoons soy sauce
- 1 tablespoon sesame seed oil
- 2 teaspoons rice vinegar
- Salt and black pepper, to taste
- Oil spray, for coating

Directions:

1. Take a small bowl and whisk together the grapeseed oil, ginger and garlic paste, sesame seed oil, rice vinegar, and soy sauce.
2. Take a large bowl and mix the chicken pieces with the prepared marinade.
3. Let it sit for 1 hour.
4. Lightly grease the broccoli with oil spray and season it with salt and black pepper.
5. Put the broccoli into the first basket and grease it with oil spray.
6. Place the chicken into the second basket.
7. Set zone 1 to AIR FRY mode at 350 degrees F for 8 minutes.
8. For zone 2 set to AIR FRY mode and set the time to 35 minutes at 350 degrees F.
9. To start cooking, hit the Sync button and press START/STOP button.
10. Once the cooking time is complete, take out and enjoy.

Serving Suggestion: Serve it with lemon wedges.

Variation Tip: A light oil alternative can be used as grapeseed oil.

Per Serving: Calories 588; Fat 32.1g; Sodium 457mg; Carbs 4g; Fiber 1.3 g; Sugar 1g; Protein 67.4 g

General Tso's Chicken

Prep time: 20 minutes| **Cook time:** 22 minutes| **Serves:** 4

Ingredients:

- 1 egg, large
- ⅓ cup 2 teaspoons cornstarch,
- ¼ teaspoons salt
- ¼ teaspoons ground white pepper
- 7 tablespoons chicken broth
- 2 tablespoons soy sauce
- 2 tablespoons ketchup
- 2 teaspoons sugar
- 2 teaspoons unseasoned rice vinegar
- 1½ tablespoons canola oil
- 4 chile de árbol, chopped and seeds discarded
- 1 tablespoon chopped fresh ginger
- 1 tablespoon garlic, chopped
- 2 tablespoons green onion, sliced
- 1 teaspoon toasted sesame oil
- 1 lb. boneless chicken thighs, cut into 1 ¼ -inch chunks
- ½ teaspoon toasted sesame seeds

Directions:

1. Add egg to a large bowl and beat it with a fork.
2. Add chicken to the egg and coat it well.
3. Whisk ⅓ cup of cornstarch with black pepper and salt in a small bowl.
4. Add chicken to the cornstarch mixture and mix well to coat.
5. Divide the chicken in the two crisper plates and spray them cooking oi.
6. Return the crisper plates to the Ninja Foodi 2-Basket Air Fryer.

7. Choose the Air Fry mode for Zone 1 and set the temperature to 390 degrees F and the time to 20 minutes.
8. Select the "MATCH" button to copy the settings for Zone 2.
9. Initiate cooking by pressing the START/STOP button.
10. Once done, remove the air fried chicken from the air fryer.
11. Whisk 2 teaspoons of cornstarch with soy sauce, broth, sugar, ketchup, and rice vinegar in a small bowl.
12. Add chilies and canola oil to a skillet and sauté for 1 minute.
13. Add garlic and ginger, then sauté for 30 seconds.
14. Stir in cornstarch sauce and cook until it bubbles and thickens.
15. Toss in cooked chicken and garnish with sesame oil, sesame seeds, and green onion.
16. Enjoy.

Serving Suggestion: Serve with boiled white rice or chow Mein.

Variation Tip: You can use honey instead of sugar to sweeten the sauce.

Per Serving: Calories 351; Fat 16g; Sodium 777mg; Carbs 26g; Fiber 4g; Sugar 5g; Protein 28g

Spicy Chicken

Prep time: 12 minutes| **Cook time:** 35-40 minutes| **Serves:** 4

Ingredients:

- 4 chicken thighs
- 2 cups buttermilk
- 4 chicken legs
- 2 cups flour
- Salt and black pepper, to taste
- 2 tablespoons garlic powder
- ½ teaspoon onion powder
- 1 teaspoon poultry seasoning
- 1 teaspoon cumin
- 2 tablespoons Paprika
- 1 tablespoon olive oil

Directions:

1. Take a bowl and add the buttermilk to it.
2. Soak the chicken thighs and chicken legs in the buttermilk for 2 hours.
3. Mix the flour, all the seasonings, and olive oil in a small bowl.
4. Take out the chicken pieces from the buttermilk mixture and then dredge them into the flour mixture.
5. Repeat the step for all the pieces and then arrange them in both the air fryer baskets.
6. Set the timer for both the baskets to ROAST mode for 35-40 minutes at 350 degrees F.
7. Once the cooking cycle is complete take them out and serve hot.

Serving Suggestion: Serve the chicken with garlic dipping sauce.

Variation Tip: Use canola oil instead of olive oil.

Per Serving: Calories 624; Fat 17.6g; Sodium 300mg; Carbs 60g; Fiber 3.5g; Sugar 7.7g; Protein 54.2g

Crumbed Chicken Katsu

Prep time: 15 minutes| **Cook time:** 26 minutes| **Serves:** 4

Ingredients:

- 1 lb. boneless chicken breast, cut in half
- 2 large eggs, beaten
- 1 ½ cups panko bread crumbs
- Salt and black pepper ground to taste
- Cooking spray

Sauce:

- 1 tablespoon sugar
- 2 tablespoons soy sauce
- 1 tablespoon sherry
- ½ cup ketchup
- 2 teaspoons Worcestershire sauce
- 1 teaspoon garlic, minced

Directions:

1. Mix soy sauce, ketchup, sherry, sugar, garlic, and Worcestershire sauce in a mixing bowl.
2. Keep this katsu aside for a while.
3. Rub the chicken pieces with salt and black pepper.
4. Whisk eggs in a shallow dish and spread breadcrumbs in another tray.
5. Dip the chicken in the egg mixture and coat them with breadcrumbs.
6. Place the coated chicken in the two crisper plates and spray them with cooking spray.
7. Return the crisper plate to the Ninja Foodi 2-Basket Air Fryer.
8. Choose the Air Fry mode for Zone 1 and set the temperature to 390 degrees F and the time to 26 minutes.
9. Select the "MATCH" button to copy the settings for Zone 2.
10. Initiate cooking by pressing the START/STOP button.
11. Flip the chicken once cooked halfway through, then resume cooking.
12. Serve warm with the sauce.

Serving Suggestion: Serve with fried rice and green beans salad.

Variation Tip: Coat the chicken with crushed cornflakes for extra crispiness.

Per Serving: Calories 220; Fat 1.7g; Sodium 178mg; Carbs 1.7g; Fiber 0.2g; Sugar 0.2g; Protein 32.9g

Pickled Chicken Fillets

Prep time: 15 minutes| **Cook time:** 28 minutes| **Serves:** 4

Ingredients:

- 2 boneless chicken breasts
- ½ cup dill pickle juice
- 2 eggs
- ½ cup milk
- 1 cup flour, all-purpose
- 2 tablespoons powdered sugar
- 2 tablespoons potato starch
- 1 teaspoon paprika
- 1 teaspoon of sea salt
- ½ teaspoon black pepper
- ½ teaspoon garlic powder

- ¼ teaspoon ground celery seed ground
- 1 tablespoon olive oil
- Cooking spray
- 4 hamburger buns, toasted
- 8 dill pickle chips

Directions:

1. Set the chicken in a suitable ziplock bag and pound it into ½ thickness with a mallet.
2. Slice the chicken into 2 halves.
3. Add pickle juice and seal the bag.
4. Refrigerate for 30 minutes approximately for marination. Whisk both eggs with milk in a shallow bowl.
5. Thoroughly mix flour with spices and flour in a separate bowl.
6. Dip each chicken slice in egg, then in the flour mixture.
7. Shake off the excess and set the chicken pieces in the crisper plate.
8. Spray the pieces with cooking oil.
9. Place the chicken pieces in the two crisper plate in a single layer and spray the cooking oil.
10. Return the crisper plate to the Ninja Foodi 2-Basket Air Fryer.
11. Choose the Air Fry mode for Zone 1 and set the temperature to 390 degrees F and the time to 28 minutes.
12. Select the "MATCH" button to copy the settings for Zone 2.
13. Initiate cooking by pressing the START/STOP button.
14. Flip the chicken pieces once cooked halfway through, and resume cooking.
15. Enjoy with pickle chips and a dollop of mayonnaise.

Serving Suggestion: Serve with warm corn tortilla and Greek salad.

Variation Tip: You can use the almond flour breading for low-carb serving.

Per Serving: Calories 353; Fat 5g; Sodium 818mg; Carbs 53.2g; Fiber 4.4g; Sugar 8g; Protein 17.3g

Chicken Breast Strips

Prep time: 10 minutes| **Cook time:** 22 minutes| **Serves:** 2

Ingredients:

- 2 large organic eggs
- 1 ounce buttermilk
- 1 cup cornmeal
- ¼ cup all-purpose flour
- Salt and black pepper, to taste
- 1 pound chicken breasts, cut into strips
- 2 tablespoons oil bay seasoning
- Oil spray, for greasing

Directions:

1. Take a medium bowl and whisk the eggs with buttermilk.
2. In a separate large bowl, mix flour, cornmeal, salt, black pepper, and oil bay seasoning.
3. First, dip the chicken breast strip in egg wash and then dredge into the flour mixture.
4. Grease the air fryer baskets and divide the chicken strips into them.
5. Set the zone 1 basket to AIR FRY mode at 400 degrees F for 22 minutes.
6. Select the MATCH button for zone 2.
7. Hit the START/STOP button to let the cooking start.
8. Once the cooking cycle is done, serve.

Serving Suggestion: Serve it with roasted vegetables.

Variation Tip: None.

Per Serving: Calories 788; Fat 25g; Sodium 835 mg; Carbs 60g; Fiber 4.9g; Sugar 1.5g; Protein 79g

Balsamic Duck Breast

Prep time: 15 minutes | **Cook time:** 20 minutes | **Serves:** 2

Ingredients:

- 2 duck breasts
- 1 teaspoon parsley
- Salt and black pepper, to taste

Marinade:

- 1 tablespoon olive oil
- ½ teaspoon French mustard
- 1 teaspoon dried garlic
- 2 teaspoons honey
- ½ teaspoon balsamic vinegar

Directions:

1. Mix olive oil, mustard, garlic, honey, and balsamic vinegar in a bowl.
2. Add duck breasts to the marinade and rub well.
3. Place one duck breast in each crisper plate.
4. Return the crisper plates to the Ninja Foodi 2-Basket Air Fryer.
5. Choose the Air Fry mode for Zone 1 and set the temperature to 360 degrees F and the time to 20 minutes.
6. Select the "MATCH" button to copy the settings for Zone 2.
7. Initiate cooking by pressing the START/STOP button.
8. Flip the duck breasts once cooked halfway through, then resume cooking.
9. Serve warm.

Serving Suggestion: Serve with white rice and avocado salad.

Variation Tip: Rub the duck breast with garlic cloves before seasoning.

Per Serving: Calories 546; Fat 33.1g; Sodium 1201mg; Carbs 30g; Fiber 2.4g; Sugar 9.7g; Protein 32g

Chili Chicken Wings

Prep time: 20 minutes | **Cook time:** 43 minutes | **Serves:** 4

Ingredients:

- 8 chicken wings drumettes
- cooking spray
- ⅛ cup low-fat buttermilk
- ¼ cup almond flour
- McCormick Chicken Seasoning to taste

Thai Chili Marinade

- 1 ½ tablespoons low-sodium soy sauce
- ½ teaspoon ginger, minced
- 1 ½ garlic cloves
- 1 green onion
- ½ teaspoon rice wine vinegar
- ½ tablespoon Sriracha sauce
- ½ tablespoon sesame oil

Directions:

1. Put all the Ingredients: for the marinade in the blender and blend them for 1 minute.
2. Keep this marinade aside. Pat dry the washed chicken and place it in the Ziploc bag.
3. Add buttermilk, chicken seasoning, and zip the bag.
4. Shake the bag well, then refrigerator for 30 minutes for marination.
5. Remove the chicken drumettes from the marinade, then dredge them through dry flour.
6. Spread the drumettes in the two crisper plate and spray them with cooking oil.
7. Return the crisper plate to the Ninja Foodi 2-Basket Air Fryer.
8. Choose the Air Fry mode for Zone 1 and set the temperature to 390 degrees F and the time to 43 minutes.
9. Select the "MATCH" button to copy the settings for Zone 2.
10. Initiate cooking by pressing the START/STOP button.
11. Toss the drumettes once cooked halfway through.
12. Now brush the chicken pieces with Thai chili sauce and then resume cooking.
13. Serve warm.

Serving Suggestion: Serve with warm corn tortilla and ketchup.

Variation Tip: Rub the wings with lemon or orange juice before cooking.

Per Serving: Calories 223; Fat 11.7g; Sodium 721mg; Carbs 13.6g; Fiber 0.7g; Sugar 8g; Protein 15.7g

Air Fried Turkey Breast

Prep time: 10 minutes| **Cook time:** 46 minutes| **Serves:** 4

Ingredients:

- 2 lbs. turkey breast, on the bone with skin
- ½ tablespoon olive oil
- 1 teaspoon salt
- ¼ tablespoon dry poultry seasoning

Directions:

1. Rub turkey breast with ½ tablespoons of oil.
2. Season both its sides with turkey seasoning and salt, then rub in the brush half tablespoons of oil over the skin of the turkey.
3. Divide the turkey in half and place each half in each of the crisper plate.
4. Return the crisper plate to the Ninja Foodi 2-Basket Air Fryer.
5. Choose the Air Fry mode for Zone 1 and set the temperature to 390 degrees F and the time to 46 minutes.
6. Select the "MATCH" button to copy the settings for Zone 2.
7. Initiate cooking by pressing the START/STOP button.
8. Flip the turkey once cooked halfway through, and resume cooking.
9. Slice and serve warm.

Serving Suggestion: Serve with warm corn tortilla and Greek salad.

Variation Tip: Coat and dust the turkey breast with flour after seasoning.

Per Serving: Calories 502; Fat 25g; Sodium 230mg; Carbs 1.5g; Fiber 0.2g; Sugar 0.4g; Protein 64.1g

Veggie Stuffed Chicken Breasts

Prep time: 15 minutes| **Cook time:** 10 minutes| **Serves:** 2

Ingredients:

- 4 teaspoons chili powder
- 4 teaspoons ground cumin
- 1 skinless, boneless chicken breast
- 2 teaspoons chipotle flakes
- 2 teaspoons Mexican oregano
- Salt and black pepper, to taste
- ½ red bell pepper, julienned
- ½ onion, julienned
- 1 fresh jalapeno pepper, julienned
- 2 teaspoons corn oil
- ½ lime, juiced

Directions:

1. Slice the chicken breast in half horizontally.
2. Pound each chicken breast with a mallet into ¼-inch thickness.
3. Rub the pounded chicken breast with black pepper, salt, oregano, chipotle flakes, cumin, and chili powder.
4. Add ½ of bell pepper, jalapeno, and onion on top of each chicken breast piece.
5. Roll the chicken to wrap the filling inside and insert toothpicks to seal.
6. Place the rolls in crisper plate and spray them with cooking oil.
7. Return the crisper plate to the Ninja Foodi 2-Basket Air Fryer.
8. Choose the Air Fry mode for Zone 1 and set the temperature to 360 degrees F and the time to 10 minutes.
9. Initiate cooking by pressing the START/STOP button.
10. Serve warm.

Serving Suggestion: Serve with tomato ketchup or chili sauce.

Variation Tip: Season the chicken rolls with seasoned parmesan before cooking.

Per Serving: Calories 351; Fat 11g; Sodium 150mg; Carbs 3.3g; Fiber 0.2g; Sugar 1g; Protein 33.2g

Chicken Wings

Prep time: 15 minutes| **Cook time:** 20 minutes| **Serves:** 3

Ingredients:

- 1 cup chicken batter mix, Louisiana
- 9 chicken wings
- ½ teaspoon smoked Paprika
- 2 tablespoons Dijon mustard
- 1 tablespoon cayenne pepper
- 1 teaspoon meat tenderizer, powder
- Oil spray, for greasing

Directions:

1. Pat dry the chicken wings and add mustard, paprika, meat tenderizer, and cayenne pepper.
2. Dredge the wings in the chicken batter mix.
3. Oil spray the chicken wings.
4. Grease both baskets of the air fryer.
5. Divide the wings between the two zones of the air fryer.

6. Set zone 1 to AIR FRY mode at 400 degrees F for 20 minutes.
7. Select MATCH for zone 2.
8. Hit START/STOP button to begin the cooking.
9. Once the cooking cycle is complete, serve, and enjoy hot.

Serving Suggestion: Serve the wings with salad.

Variation Tip: Use American yellow mustard instead of Dijon mustard.

Per Serving: Calories 621; Fat 32.6g; Sodium 2016mg; Carbs 46.6g; Fiber 1.1g; Sugar 0.2g; Protein 32.1g

Spice-Rubbed Chicken Pieces

Prep time: 22 minutes| **Cook time:** 40 minutes| **Serves:** 6

Ingredients:

- 3 pounds chicken, pieces
- 1 teaspoon sweet Paprika
- 1 teaspoon mustard powder
- 1 tablespoon dark brown sugar
- Salt and black pepper, to taste
- 1 teaspoon chile powder, New Mexico
- 1 teaspoon oregano, dried
- ¼ teaspoon all-spice powder

Directions:

1. In a bowl and mix in the brown sugar, salt, paprika, mustard powder, oregano, chile powder, black pepper, and All Spice powder.
2. Mix well and rub this spice mixture all over the chicken.
3. Divide the chicken between two air fryer baskets.
4. Oil spray the meat and then add it to the air fryer.
5. Now press button 1 and set the time to 40 minutes at 350 degrees F.
6. Press MATCH and START/STOP for the cooking process to begin.
7. Once the cooking cycle is complete, press START/STOP for both the zones.
8. Take out the chicken and serve hot.

Serving Suggestion: Serve it with coleslaw, peanut sauce, or ranch.

Variation Tip: Use light brown sugar instead of dark brown sugar.

Per Serving: Calories 353; Fat 7.1g; Sodium 400mg; Carbs 2.2g; Fiber 0.4g; Sugar 1.6g; Protein 66g

Chicken Potatoes

Prep time: 10 minutes| **Cook time:** 22 minutes| **Serves:** 4

Ingredients:

- 15 ounces canned potatoes drained
- 1 teaspoon olive oil
- 1 teaspoon Lawry's seasoned salt
- ⅛ teaspoons black pepper optional
- 8 ounces boneless chicken breast cubed
- ¼ teaspoon paprika
- ⅜ cup cheddar, shredded
- 4 bacon slices, cooked, cut into strips

Directions:

1. Dice the chicken into small pieces and toss them with olive oil and spices.
2. Drain and dice the potato pieces into smaller cubes.
3. Add potato to the chicken and mix well to coat.
4. Spread the mixture in the two crisper plates in a single layer.
5. Return the crisper plates to the Ninja Foodi 2-Basket Air Fryer.
6. Choose the Air Fry mode for Zone 1 and set the temperature to 390 degrees F and the time to 22 minutes.
7. Select the "MATCH" button to copy the settings for Zone 2.
8. Initiate cooking by pressing the START/STOP button.
9. Top the chicken and potatoes with cheese and bacon.
10. Return the crisper plates to the Ninja Foodi 2-Basket Air Fryer.
11. Select the Max Crisp mode for Zone 1 and set the temperature to 300 degrees F and the time to 5 minutes.
12. Initiate cooking by pressing the START/STOP button.
13. Repeat the same step for Zone 2 to broil the potatoes and chicken in the right drawer.
14. Enjoy with dried herbs on top.

Serving Suggestion: Serve with boiled white rice.

Variation Tip: Add sweet potatoes and green beans instead of potatoes.

Per Serving: Calories 346; Fat 16.1g; Sodium 882mg; Carbs 1.3g; Fiber 0.5g; Sugar 0.5g; Protein 48.2g

Yummy Chicken Breasts

Prep time: 15 minutes| **Cook time:** 25 minutes| **Serves:** 2

Ingredients:

- 4 large chicken breasts, 6 ounces each
- 2 tablespoons oil bay seasoning
- 1 tablespoon Montreal chicken seasoning
- 1 teaspoon thyme
- ½ teaspoon Paprika
- Salt, to taste
- Oil spray, for greasing

Directions:

1. Season the chicken breast pieces with the listed seasoning and let them rest for 40 minutes.
2. Grease both sides of the chicken breast pieces with oil spray.
3. Divide the pieces between both baskets.
4. Set zone 1 to AIR FRY mode at 400 degrees F for 15 minutes.
5. Select the MATCH button for zone 2 basket.
6. Press START/STOP and take out the baskets and flip the chicken breast pieces.
7. Select the zones to 400 degrees F for 10 more minutes using the MATCH button.
8. Once it's done serve and enjoy.

Serving Suggestion: Serve with baked potato.

Variation Tip: None.

Per Serving: Calories 711; Fat 27.7g; Sodium 895mg; Carbs 1.6g; Fiber 0.4g; Sugar 0.1g; Protein 106.3g

Chicken Leg Piece

Prep time: 15 minutes| **Cook time:** 25 minutes| **Serves:** 1

Ingredients:

- 1 teaspoon onion powder
- 1 teaspoon Paprika powder
- 1 teaspoon garlic powder
- Salt and black pepper, to taste
- 1 tablespoon Italian seasoning
- 1 teaspoon celery seeds
- 2 eggs, whisked
- ⅓ cup buttermilk
- 1 cup corn flour
- 1 pound chicken legs

Directions:

1. Take a bowl and whisk the eggs along with pepper, salt, and buttermilk and set aside.
2. Mix all the spices in a small separate bowl.
3. Dredge the chicken in the egg wash, then dredge it in the spice seasoning.
4. Coat the chicken legs with oil spray.
5. At the end, dust it with the corn flour.
6. Divide the leg pieces into the two zones.
7. Set zone 1 basket to 400 degrees F for 25 minutes.
8. Select MATCH for zone 2 basket.
9. Let the air fryer do the magic.
10. Once it's done, serve and enjoy.

Serving Suggestion: Serve it with cooked rice.

Variation Tip: Use water instead of buttermilk.

Per Serving: Calories 1511; Fat 52.3g; Sodium 615 mg; Carbs 100g; Fiber 9.2g; Sugar 8.1g; Protein 154.2g

Cheddar-Stuffed Chicken

Prep time: 10 minutes| **Cook time:** 20 minutes| **Serves:** 4

Ingredients:

- 3 bacon strips, cooked and crumbled
- 2 ounces Cheddar cheese, cubed
- ¼ cup barbeque sauce
- 2 (4 ounces) boneless chicken breasts
- Salt and black pepper to taste

Directions:

1. Make a 1-inch-deep pouch in each chicken breast.
2. Mix cheddar cubes with half of the BBQ sauce, salt, black pepper, and bacon.
3. Divide this filling in the chicken breasts and secure the edges with a toothpick.
4. Brush the remaining BBQ sauce over the chicken breasts.
5. Place the chicken in the crisper plate and spray them with cooking oil.
6. Return the crisper plate to the Ninja Foodi 2-Basket Air Fryer.
7. Choose the Air Fry mode for Zone 1 and set the temperature to 360 degrees F and the time to 20 minutes.
8. Initiate cooking by pressing the START/STOP button.
9. Serve warm.

Serving Suggestion: Serve with tomato salsa on top.

Variation Tip: Use poultry seasoning for breading.

Per Serving: Calories 379; Fat 19g; Sodium 184mg; Carbs 12.3g; Fiber 0.6g; Sugar 2g; Protein 37.7g

Beef, Pork, and Lamb Recipes

Beef & Broccoli

Prep time: 12 minutes| **Cook time:** 12 minutes| **Serves:** 4

Ingredients:

- 12 ounces Teriyaki sauce, divided
- ½ tablespoon garlic powder
- ¼ cup soy sauce
- 1 pound raw sirloin steak, thinly sliced
- 2 cups broccoli, cut into florets
- 2 teaspoons olive oil
- Salt and black pepper, to taste

Directions:

1. Mix the Teriyaki sauce, salt, garlic powder, black pepper, soy sauce, and olive oil in a zip-lock bag.
2. Add the beef and let it marinate for 2 hours.
3. Drain the beef from the marinade.
4. Toss the broccoli with oil, teriyaki sauce, and salt and black pepper and place in the zone 1 basket.
5. Place the beef in both baskets and set it to SYNC button.
6. Hit START/STOP button and let the cooking cycle complete.
7. Once it's done, take out the beef and broccoli and serve with the leftover Teriyaki sauce and cooked rice.

Serving Suggestion: Serve it with mashed potatoes.

Variation Tip: Use canola oil instead of olive oil.

Per Serving: Calories 344; Fat 10g; Sodium 4285mg; Carbs 18.2 g; Fiber 1.5g; Sugar 13.3g; Protein 42g

Short Ribs & Root Vegetables

Prep time: 15 minutes| **Cook time:** 45 minutes| **Serves:** 2

Ingredients:

- 1 pound beef short ribs, bone-in and trimmed
- Salt and black pepper, to taste
- 2 tablespoons canola oil, divided
- ¼ cup red wine
- 3 tablespoons brown sugar
- 2 cloves garlic, peeled, minced
- 4 carrots, peeled, cut into 1-inch pieces
- 2 parsnips, peeled, cut into 1-inch pieces
- ½ cup pearl onions

Directions:

1. Season the ribs with salt and black pepper and rub a small amount of canola oil on both sides.
2. Place the ribs in zone 1 basket of the air fryer.
3. Next, take a bowl and add the pearl onions, parsnips, carrots, garlic, brown sugar, red wine, salt, and black pepper.
4. Add the vegetable mixture to the zone 2 basket.

5. Press the Sync button.
6. Hit START/STOP button so the cooking cycle begins.
7. Once the cooking is complete, take out and serve.
8. Enjoy it hot.

Serving Suggestion: Serve it with mashed potatoes.

Variation Tip: Use olive oil instead of canola oil.

Per Serving: Calories 1262; Fat 98.6g; Sodium 595mg; Carbs 57g; Fiber 10.1g; Sugar 28.2g; Protein 35.8g

Pork Chops

Prep time: 10 minutes| **Cook time:** 17 minutes| **Serves:** 2

Ingredients:

- 1 tablespoon rosemary, chopped
- Salt and black pepper, to taste
- 2 garlic cloves
- 1 inch ginger
- 2 tablespoons olive oil
- 8 pork chops

Directions:

1. Take a blender and pulse rosemary, salt, pepper, garlic cloves, ginger, and olive oil.
2. Rub this marinade over the pork chops and let it rest for 1 hour.
3. Divide the chops into both the baskets. Set zone 1 to AIR FRY mode for 17 minutes.
4. Select the MATCH button for zone 2.
5. Once done, take out and serve hot.

Serving Suggestion: Serve with salad.

Variation Tip: Use canola oil instead of olive oil.

Per Serving: Calories 1154; Fat 93.8g; Sodium 225mg; Carbs 2.1g; Fiber0.8 g; Sugar 0g; Protein 72.2g

Glazed Steak Recipe

Prep time: 15 minutes| **Cook time:** 25 minutes| **Serves:** 2

Ingredients:

- 1 pound beef steaks
- ½ cup, soy sauce
- Salt and black pepper, to taste
- 1 tablespoon vegetable oil
- 1 teaspoon grated ginger
- 4 cloves garlic, minced
- ¼ cup brown sugar

Directions:

1. Whisk together soy sauce, salt, pepper, vegetable oil, garlic, brown sugar, and ginger in a bowl.
2. Once a paste is made from the mixture, rub the steak with it and let it sit for 30 minutes.

3. Add the steak to the air fryer basket and set it to MAX CRISP mode at 400 degrees F for 18-22 minutes.
4. After 10 minutes, hit START/STOP and take it out to flip and return to the air fryer.
5. Once the time is complete, take out the steak and let it rest. Serve by cutting into slices.
6. Enjoy.

Serving Suggestion: Serve it with mashed potatoes.

Variation Tip: Use canola oil instead of vegetable oil.

Per Serving: Calories 563; Fat 21 g; Sodium 156mg; Carbs 20.6g; Fiber 0.3 g; Sugar 17.8 g; Protein 69.4 g

Beef Ribs I

Prep time: 10 minutes| **Cook time:** 15 minutes| **Serves:** 2

Ingredients:

- 4 tablespoons BBQ spice rub
- 1 tablespoon kosher salt and black pepper
- 3 tablespoons brown sugar
- 2 pounds beef ribs cut in thirds
- 1 cup BBQ sauce
- Oil spray

Directions:

1. In a small bowl, add salt, pepper, brown sugar, and BBQ spice rub.
2. Grease the ribs with oil spray from both sides and then rub it with BBQ the spice.
3. Divide the ribs into both baskets and set zone 1to AIR FRY mode at 375 degrees F for 15 minutes.
4. Press MATCH for zone 2.
5. Hit START/STOP button and let the air fryer cook the ribs.
6. Once done, serve with a coating BBQ sauce.

Serving Suggestion: Serve it with salad and baked potato.

Variation Tip: Use sea salt instead of kosher salt.

Per Serving: Calories 1081; Fat 28.6 g; Sodium 1701mg; Carbs 58g; Fiber 0.8g; Sugar 45.7g; Protein 138 g

Beef Ribs II

Prep time: 20 minutes| **Cook time: 1** Hour | **Serves:** 2

Ingredients:

for Marinade:

- ¼ cup olive oil
- 4 garlic cloves, minced
- ½ cup white wine vinegar
- ¼ cup soy sauce, reduced-sodium
- ¼ cup Worcestershire sauce
- 1 lemon juice
- Salt and black pepper, to taste
- 2 tablespoons Italian seasoning
- 1 teaspoon smoked Paprika
- 2 tablespoons mustard

- ½ cup maple syrup

Meat Ingredients:

- Oil spray, for greasing
- 8 beef ribs lean

Directions:

1. Take a large bowl and add all the marinade Ingredients: and mix well then place into a zip lock bag along with the ribs. Let it sit for 4 hours.
2. Grease the air fryer baskets and divide the ribs into them.
3. Set zone 1 to AIR FRY mode at 220 degrees F for 30 minutes.
4. Select MATCH button for zone 2.
5. After the time is up, select START/STOP and take out the baskets.
6. Flip the ribs and cook for 30 more minutes at 250 degrees F.
7. Once done, serve the juicy and tender ribs.
8. Enjoy.

Serving Suggestion: Serve it with mac and cheese

Variation Tip: Use garlic-infused oil instead of garlic cloves

Per Serving: Calories 1927; Fat 116g; Sodium 1394mg; Carbs 35.2g; Fiber 1.3g; Sugar29 g; Protein 172.3g

Chinese BBQ Pork

Prep time: 15 minutes| **Cook time:** 25-35 minutes| **Serves:** 2

Ingredients:

- 4 tablespoons soy sauce
- ¼ cup red wine
- 2 tablespoons oyster sauce
- ¼ tablespoon hoisin sauce
- ¼ cup honey
- ¼ cup brown sugar
- Pinch of salt
- Pinch of black pepper
- 1 teaspoon ginger garlic, paste
- 1 teaspoon five-spice powder

Other Ingredients:

- 1.5 pounds pork shoulder, sliced

Directions:

1. Take a bowl and mix all the sauce Ingredients: well.
2. Transfer half of it to a sauce pan and cook for 10 minutes, and then set it aside.
3. Let the pork marinate in the remaining sauce for 2 hours.
4. Place the pork slices in the air fryer basket in zone 1 and set it to AIR FRY mode at 450 degrees F for 25 minutes.
5. Make sure the internal temperature is above 160 degrees F once cooked.
6. If not, add a few more minutes to the overall cooking time.
7. Once done, take it out and baste it with the cooked sauce.
8. Serve and Enjoy.

Serving Suggestion: Serve it with rice.

Variation Tip: Skip the wine and add vinegar.

Per Serving: Calories 1239; Fat 73 g; Sodium 2185 mg; Carbs 57.3 g; Fiber 0.4g; Sugar 53.7 g; Protein 81.5 g

Pork Chops with Brussels Sprouts

Prep time: 15 minutes| **Cook time:** 15 minutes | **Serves:** 4

Ingredients:

- 4 bone-in center-cut pork chop
- Cooking spray
- Salt, to taste
- Black pepper, to taste
- 2 teaspoons olive oil
- 2 teaspoons pure maple syrup
- 2 teaspoons Dijon mustard
- 6 ounces Brussels sprouts, quartered

Directions:

1. Rub pork chop with salt, ¼ teaspoons black pepper, and cooking spray.
2. Toss Brussels sprouts with mustard, syrup, oil, ¼ teaspoon of black pepper in a medium bowl.
3. Add pork chop to the crisper plate of Zone 1 of the Ninja Foodi 2-Basket Air Fryer.
4. Return the crisper plate to the Ninja Foodi 2-Basket Air Fryer.
5. Choose the Air Fry mode for Zone 1 and set the temperature to 400 degrees F and the time to 15 minutes.
6. Add the Brussels sprouts to the crisper plate of Zone 2 and return it to the unit.
7. Choose the Air Fry mode for Zone 2 with 350 degrees F and the time to 13 minutes.
8. Press the SYNC button to sync the finish time for both Zones.
9. Initiate cooking by pressing the START/STOP button.
10. Serve warm and fresh.

Serving Suggestion: Serve with Greek salad and crispy bread.

Variation Tip: Rub the pork chops with garlic cloves before seasoning.

Per Serving: Calories 336; Fat 27.1g; Sodium 66mg; Carbs 1.1g; Fiber 0.4g; Sugar 0.2g; Protein 19.7g

Chipotle Beef

Prep time: 15 minutes| **Cook time:** 18 minutes | **Serves:** 4

Ingredients:

- 1 lb. beef steak, cut into chunks
- 1 large egg
- ½ cup parmesan cheese, grated
- ½ cup pork panko
- ½ teaspoon seasoned salt

Chipotle Ranch Dip
- ¼ cup mayonnaise
- ¼ cup sour cream
- 1 teaspoon chipotle paste
- ½ teaspoon ranch dressing mix
- ¼ medium lime, juiced

Directions:

1. Mix all the Ingredients: for chipotle ranch dip in a bowl.

2. Keep it in the refrigerator for 30 minutes.
3. Mix pork panko with salt and parmesan.
4. Beat egg in one bowl and spread the panko mixture in another flat bowl.
5. Dip the steak chunks in the egg first, then coat them with panko mixture.
6. Spread them in the two crisper plates and spray them with cooking oil.
7. Return the crisper plate to the Ninja Foodi 2-Basket Air Fryer.
8. Choose the Air Fry mode for Zone 1 and set the temperature to 390 degrees F and the time to 18 minutes.
9. Select the "MATCH" button to copy the settings for Zone 2.
10. Initiate cooking by pressing the START/STOP button.
11. Serve with chipotle ranch and salt and pepper on top. Enjoy.

Serving Suggestion: Serve with tomato ketchup or chili sauce.

Variation Tip: Add crushed cornflakes for breading to get extra crisp.

Per Serving: Calories 310; Fat 17g; Sodium 271mg; Carbs 4.3g; Fiber 0.9g; Sugar 2.1g; Protein 35g

Turkey and Beef Meatballs

Prep time: 15 minutes | **Cook time:** 24 minutes | **Serves:** 6

Ingredients:

- 1 medium shallot, minced
- 2 tablespoons olive oil
- 3 garlic cloves, minced
- ¼ cup panko crumbs
- 2 tablespoons whole milk
- ⅔ lb. lean ground beef
- ⅓ lb. bulk turkey sausage
- 1 large egg, lightly beaten
- ¼ cup parsley, chopped
- 1 tablespoon fresh thyme, chopped
- 1 tablespoon fresh rosemary, chopped
- 1 tablespoon Dijon mustard
- ½ teaspoon salt

Directions:

1. Preheat your oven to 400 degrees F. Place a medium non-stick pan over medium-high heat.
2. Add oil and shallot, then sauté for 2 minutes.
3. Toss in the garlic and cook for 1 minute.
4. Remove this pan from the heat.
5. Whisk panko with milk in a large bowl and leave it for 5 minutes.
6. Add cooked shallot mixture and mix well.
7. Stir in egg, parsley, turkey sausage, beef, thyme, rosemary, salt, and mustard.
8. Mix well, then divide the mixture into 1 ½-inch balls.
9. Divide these balls into the two crisper plates and spray them with cooking oil.
10. Return the crisper plates to the Ninja Foodi 2-Basket Air Fryer.
11. Choose the Air Fry mode for Zone 1 and set the temperature to 400 degrees F and the time to 21 minutes.
12. Select the "MATCH" button to copy the settings for Zone 2.
13. Initiate cooking by pressing the START/STOP button.
14. Serve warm.

Serving Suggestion: Serve with fresh vegetable salad and marinara sauce.

Variation Tip: Add freshly chopped parsley and coriander for change of taste.

Per Serving: Calories 551; Fat 31g; Sodium 1329mg; Carbs 1.5g; Fiber 0.8g; Sugar 0.4g; Protein 64g

Pork with Green Beans and Potatoes

Prep time: 10 minutes | **Cook time:** 15 minutes | **Serves:** 4

Ingredients:

- ¼ cup Dijon mustard
- 2 tablespoons brown sugar
- 1 teaspoon dried parsley flake
- ½ teaspoon dried thyme
- ¼ teaspoons salt
- ¼ teaspoons black pepper
- 1 ¼ lbs. pork tenderloin
- ¾ lb. small potatoes halved
- 1 (12-oz) package green beans, trimmed
- 1 tablespoon olive oil
- Salt and black pepper ground to taste

Directions:

1. Preheat your Air Fryer Machine to 400 degrees F.
2. Add mustard, parsley, brown sugar, salt, black pepper, and thyme in a large bowl, then mix well.
3. Add tenderloin to the spice mixture and coat well.
4. Toss potatoes with olive oil, salt, black pepper, and green beans in another bowl.
5. Place the prepared tenderloin in the crisper plate.
6. Return this crisper plate to the Zone 1 of the Ninja Foodi 2-Basket Air Fryer.
7. Choose the Air Fry mode for Zone 1 and set the temperature to 390 degrees F and the time to 15 minutes.
8. Add potatoes and green beans to the Zone 2.
9. Choose the Air Fry mode for Zone 2 with 350 degrees F and the time to 10 minutes.
10. Press the SYNC button to sync the finish time for both Zones.
11. Initiate cooking by pressing the START/STOP button.
12. Serve the tenderloin with Air Fried potatoes

Serving Suggestion: Serve with sautéed leeks or cabbages.

Variation Tip: Rub the tenderloins with garlic cloves before seasoning.

Per Serving: Calories 400; Fat 32g; Sodium 721mg; Carbs 2.6g; Fiber 0g; Sugar 0g; Protein 27.4g

Zucchini Pork Skewers

Prep time: 15 minutes | **Cook time:** 23 minutes | **Serves:** 4

Ingredients:

- 1 large zucchini, cut 1" pieces
- 1 lb. boneless pork belly, cut into cubes
- 1 onion yellow, diced in squares
- 1 ½ cups grape tomatoes
- 1 garlic clove minced
- 1 lemon, juice only
- ¼ cup olive oil
- 2 tablespoons balsamic vinegar
- 1 teaspoon oregano
- olive oil spray

Directions:

1. Mix together balsamic vinegar, garlic, oregano lemon juice, and ¼ cup of olive oil in a suitable bowl.
2. Then toss in diced pork pieces and mix well to coat.
3. Leave the seasoned pork to marinate for 60 minutes in the refrigerator.
4. Take suitable wooden skewers for your Ninja Foodi 2-Basket Air Fryer's drawer, and then thread marinated pork and vegetables on each skewer in an alternating manner.
5. Place half of the skewers in each of the crisper plate and spray them with cooking oil.
6. Return the crisper plate to the Ninja Foodi 2-Basket Air Fryer.
7. Choose the Air Fry mode for Zone 1 and set the temperature to 390 degrees F and the time to 23 minutes.
8. Select the "MATCH" button to copy the settings for Zone 2.
9. Initiate cooking by pressing the START/STOP button.
10. Flip the skewers once cooked halfway through, and resume cooking.
11. Serve warm.

Serving Suggestion: Serve with sautéed green beans and cherry tomatoes.

Variation Tip: Use honey glaze to baste the skewers.

Per Serving: Calories 459; Fat 17.7g; Sodium 1516mg; Carbs 1.7g; Fiber 0.5g; Sugar 0.4g; Protein 69.2g

Air Fryer Meatloaves

Prep time: 10 minutes | **Cook time:** 22 minutes | **Serves:** 4

Ingredients:

- ⅓ cup milk
- 2 tablespoons basil pesto
- 1 egg, beaten
- 1 garlic clove, minced
- ¼ teaspoons black pepper
- 1 lb. ground beef
- ⅓ cup panko bread crumbs
- 8 pepperoni slices
- ½ cup marinara sauce, warmed
- 1 tablespoon fresh basil, chopped

Directions:

1. Mix pesto, milk, egg, garlic, and black pepper in a medium-sized bowl.
2. Stir in ground beef and bread crumbs, then mix.
3. Make the 4 small-sized loaves with this mixture and top them with 2 pepperoni slices.
4. Press the slices into the meatloaves.
5. Place the meatloaves in the two crisper plates.
6. Return the crisper plate to the Ninja Foodi 2-Basket Air Fryer.
7. Choose the Air Fry mode for Zone 1 and set the temperature to 390 degrees F and the time to 22 minutes.
8. Select the "MATCH" button to copy the settings for Zone 2.
9. Initiate cooking by pressing the START/STOP button.
10. Top them with marinara sauce and basil to serve.
11. Serve warm.

Serving Suggestion: Serve with avocado dip.

Variation Tip: Add finely chopped carrots and zucchini to the meatloaf.

Per Serving: Calories 316; Fat 12.2g; Sodium 587mg; Carbs 12.2g; Fiber 1g; Sugar 1.8g; Protein 25.8g

Spicy Lamb Chops

Prep time: 15 minutes| **Cook time:** 15 minutes| **Serves:** 4

Ingredients:

- 12 lamb chops, bone-in
- Salt and black pepper, to taste
- ½ teaspoon lemon zest
- 1 tablespoon lemon juice
- 1 teaspoon paprika
- 1 teaspoon garlic powder
- ½ teaspoon Italian seasoning
- ¼ teaspoon onion powder

Directions:

1. Add the lamb chops to the bowl and sprinkle with salt, garlic powder, Italian seasoning, onion powder, black pepper, lemon zest, lemon juice, and paprika.
2. Rub the chops well, and divide them between both the baskets of the air fryer.
3. Set zone 1 basket to 400 degrees F, for 15 minutes on AIR FRY mode.
4. Select MATCH for zone 2 basket.
5. After 10 minutes, take out the baskets and flip the chops. Cook for the remaining minutes, and then serve.

Serving Suggestion: Serve it over rice.

Variation Tip: None.

Per Serving: Calories 787; Fat 45.3g; Sodium 1mg; Carbs 16.1g; Fiber 0.3g; Sugar 0.4g; Protein 75.3g

Dessert Recipes

Mini Blueberry Pies

Prep time: 12 minutes| **Cook time:** 10minutes | **Serves:** 2

Ingredients:

- 1 box store-bought pie dough, Trader Joe's
- ¼ cup blueberry jam
- 1 teaspoon lemon zest
- 1 egg white, for brushing

Directions:

1. Take the store-bought pie dough and cut it into 3-inch circles.
2. Brush the dough with egg white all around the edges.
3. Now add blueberry jam and zest in the middle and top it with another circle.
4. Press the edges with a fork to seal it.
5. Make a slit in the middle of each pie and divide them between the baskets.
6. Set zone 1 to AIR FRY mode 360 degrees for 10 minutes.
7. Select the MATCH button for zone 2.
8. Once cooked, serve.

Serving Suggestion: Serve it with vanilla ice-cream.

Variation Tip: Use orange zest instead of lemon zest.

Per Serving: Calories 234; Fa t8.6g; Sodium 187 mg; Carbs 38.2 g; Fiber 0.1g; Sugar 13.7g; Protein 2g

Lemony Sweet Twists

Prep time: 15 minutes| **Cook time:** 9 minutes | **Serves:** 2

Ingredients:

- 1 box store-bought puff pastry
- ½ teaspoon lemon zest
- 1 tablespoon lemon juice
- 2 teaspoons brown sugar
- Salt, pinch
- 2 tablespoons Parmesan cheese, freshly grated

Directions:

1. Put the puff pastry dough on a clean work surface.
2. In a bowl, combine Parmesan cheese, brown sugar, salt, lemon zest, and lemon juice.
3. Press this mixture into both sides of the dough.
4. Now, cut the pastry into 1" x 4" strips.
5. Twist 2 times from each end.
6. Place the strips into the air fryer baskets.
7. Select zone 1 to AIR FRY mode at 400 degrees F for 9-10 minutes.
8. Select MATCH for zone 2 basket.
9. Once cooked, serve and enjoy.

Serving Suggestion: Serve them with champagne.

Variation Tip: None

Per Serving: Calories 156; Fat 10g; Sodium 215mg; Carbs 14g; Fiber 0.4g; Sugar 3.3g; Protein 2.8g

Biscuit Doughnuts

Prep time: 15 minutes| **Cook time:** 15 minutes | **Serves:** 8

Ingredients:

- ½ cup white sugar
- 1 teaspoon cinnamon
- ½ cup powdered sugar
- 1 can pre-made biscuit dough
- Coconut oil
- Melted butter to brush biscuits

Directions:

1. Place all the biscuits on a cutting board and cut holes in the center of each biscuit using a cookie cutter.
2. Grease the crisper plate with coconut oil.
3. Place the biscuits in the two crisper plates while keeping them 1 inch apart.
4. Return the crisper plates to the Ninja Foodi 2-Basket Air Fryer.
5. Choose the Air Fry mode for Zone 1 and set the temperature to 375 degrees F and the time to 15 minutes.
6. Select the "MATCH" button to copy the settings for Zone 2.
7. Initiate cooking by pressing the START/STOP button.
8. Brush all the donuts with melted butter and sprinkle cinnamon and sugar on top.
9. Air fry these donuts for one minute more.
10. Enjoy!

Serving Suggestion: Serve the doughnuts with chocolate syrup on top.

Variation Tip: Inject strawberry jam into each doughnut.

Per Serving: Calories 192; Fat 9.3g; Sodium 133mg; Carbs 27.1g; Fiber 1.4g; Sugar 19g; Protein 3.2g

Fudge Brownies

Prep time: 20 minutes| **Cook time:** 16 minutes | **Serves:** 4

Ingredients:

- ½ cup all-purpose flour
- ¼ cup unsweetened cocoa powder
- ¾ teaspoon kosher salt
- 2 large eggs, whisked
- 1 tablespoon almond milk
- ½ cup brown sugar
- ½ cup packed white sugar
- ½ tablespoon vanilla extract
- 8 ounces semisweet chocolate chips, melted
- ½ cup unsalted butter, melted

Directions:

1. Take a medium bowl, and use a hand beater to whisk together eggs, milk, both the sugars and vanilla.
2. In a separate microwave-safe bowl, mix the melted butter and chocolate and microwave it for 30 seconds to melt the chocolate.

3. Add all the dry Ingredients: to the chocolate mixture.
4. Slowly add the egg mixture to the bowl.
Spray a reasonable round baking pan and pour the batter into the pan.
5. Select the AIR FRY mode and adjust the setting the temperature to 300 degrees F, for 30 minutes.
6. Check it after 30 minutes and if not done, cook for 10 more minutes.
7. Once it's done, take it out and let it cool before serving.
8. Enjoy.

Serving Suggestion: Serve it with a dollop of the vanilla ice cream.

Variation Tip: Use dairy milk instead of almond milk.

Per Serving: Calories 760; Fat 43.3 g; Sodium 644mg; Carbs 93.2g; Fiber 5.3g; Sugar 70.2g; Protein 6.2g

Walnuts Fritters

Prep time: 15 minutes| **Cook time:** 15 minutes | **Serves:** 6

Ingredients:

- 1 cup all-purpose flour
- ½ cup walnuts, chopped
- ¼ cup white sugar
- ¼ cup milk
- 1 egg
- 1 ½ teaspoons baking powder
- 1 pinch salt
- Cooking spray
- 2 tablespoons white sugar
- ½ teaspoon ground cinnamon

Glaze:

- ½ cup confectioners' sugar
- 1 tablespoon milk
- ½ teaspoon caramel extract
- ¼ teaspoons ground cinnamon

Directions:

1. Layer both crisper plate with parchment paper.
2. Grease the parchment paper with cooking spray.
3. Whisk flour with milk, ¼ cup of sugar, egg, baking powder, and salt in a small bowl.
4. Separately mix 2 tablespoons of sugar with cinnamon in another bowl, toss in walnuts and mix well to coat.
5. Stir in flour mixture and mix until combined.
6. Drop the fritters mixture using a cookie scoop into the two crisper plate.
7. Return the crisper plate to the Ninja Foodi 2-Basket Air Fryer.
8. Choose the Air Fry mode for Zone 1 and set the temperature to 375 degrees F and the time to 15 minutes.
9. Select the "MATCH" button to copy the settings for Zone 2.
10. Initiate cooking by pressing the START/STOP button.
11. Flip the fritters once cooked halfway through, then resume cooking.
12. Meanwhile, whisk milk, caramel extract, confectioners' sugar, and cinnamon in a bowl.
13. Transfer fritters to a wire rack and allow them to cool.
14. Drizzle with a glaze over the fritters.

Serving Suggestion: Serve with butter pecan ice cream or strawberry jam.

Variation Tip: Add maple syrup on top.

Per Serving: Calories 391; Fat 24g; Sodium 142mg; Carbs 38.5g; Fiber 3.5g; Sugar 21g; Protein 6.6g

Air Fryer Sweet Twists

Prep time: 15 minutes| **Cook time:** 9 minutes | **Serves:** 2

Ingredients:

- 1 box store-bought puff pastry
- ½ teaspoon cinnamon
- ½ teaspoon sugar
- ½ teaspoon black sesame seeds
- Salt, pinch
- 2 tablespoons Parmesan cheese, freshly grated

Directions:

1. Place the dough on a work surface.
2. Take a small bowl and mix in cheese, sugar, salt, sesame seeds, and cinnamon.
3. Press this mixture on both sides of the dough.
4. Now, cut the pastry into 1" x 3" strips.
5. Twist each of the strips twice from each end.
6. Transfer them to both the air fryer baskets.
7. Select zone 1 to AIR FRY mode at 400 degrees F for 9-10 minutes.
8. Select the MATCH button for the zone 2 basket.
9. Once cooked, serve.

Serving Suggestion: Serve it with champagne.

Variation Tip: None

Per Serving: Calories 140; Fat9.4g; Sodium 142mg; Carbs 12.3g; Fiber 0.8 g; Sugar 1.2g; Protein 2g

Chocolate Chip Cake

Prep time: 12 minutes| **Cook time:** 15 minutes | **Serves:** 4

Ingredients:

- Salt, pinch
- 2 eggs, whisked
- ½ cup brown sugar
- ½ cup butter, melted
- 10 tablespoons almond milk
- ¼ teaspoon vanilla extract
- ½ teaspoon baking powder
- 1 cup all-purpose flour
- 1 cup chocolate chips
- ½ cup cocoa powder

Directions:

1. Take 2 round baking pans that fit inside the baskets of the air fryer and line them with baking paper.
2. In a bowl with an electric beater, mix the eggs, brown sugar, butter, almond milk, and vanilla extract.
3. In a second bowl, mix the flour, cocoa powder, baking powder, and salt.
4. Slowly add the dry Ingredients: to the wet Ingredients.
5. Fold in the chocolate chips and mix well with a spoon or spatula.

6. Divide this batter into the round baking pans.
7. Set the time for zone 1 to 16 minutes at 350 degrees F on AIR FRY mode.
8. Select the MATCH button for the zone 2 basket.
9. After the time is up, check. If they're not done, let them AIR FRY for one more minute.
10. Once it is done, serve.

Serving Suggestion: Serve it with chocolate syrup drizzle

Variation Tip: Use baking soda instead of baking powder

Per Serving: Calories 736; Fat 45.5g; Sodium 356mg; Carbs 78.2g; Fiber 6.1g; Sugar 32.7g; Protein 11.5 g

Apple Hand Pies

Prep time: 15 minutes| **Cook time:** 21 minutes | **Serves:** 8

Ingredients:

- 8 tablespoons butter, softened
- 12 tablespoons brown sugar
- 2 teaspoons cinnamon, ground
- 4 medium Granny Smith apples, diced
- 2 teaspoons cornstarch
- 4 teaspoons cold water
- 1 (14-oz) package pastry, 9-inch crust pie
- Cooking spray
- 1 tablespoon grapeseed oil
- ½ cup powdered sugar
- 2 teaspoons milk

Directions:

1. Toss apples with brown sugar, butter, and cinnamon in a suitable skillet.
2. Place the skillet over medium heat and stir cook for 5 minutes.
3. Mix cornstarch with cold water in a small bowl.
4. Add cornstarch mixture into the apple and cook for 1 minute until it thickens.
5. Remove this filling from the heat and allow it to cool.
6. Unroll the pie crust and spray on a floured surface.
7. Cut the dough into 16 equal rectangles.
8. Wet the edges of the 8 rectangles with water and divide the apple filling at the center of these rectangles.
9. Place the other 8 rectangles on top and crimp the edges with a fork, then make 2-3 slashes on top.
10. Place 4 small pies in each of the crisper plate.
11. Return the crisper plate to the Ninja Foodi 2-Basket Air Fryer.
12. Choose the Air Fry mode for Zone 1 and set the temperature to 390 degrees F and the time to 17 minutes.
13. Select the "MATCH" button to copy the settings for Zone 2.
14. Initiate cooking by pressing the START/STOP button.
15. Flip the pies once cooked halfway through, and resume cooking.
16. Meanwhile, mix sugar with milk.
17. Pour this mixture over the apple pies.
18. Serve fresh.

Serving Suggestion: Serve with apple sauce.

Variation Tip: Add shredded nuts and coconuts to the filling.

Per Serving: Calories 284; Fat 16g; Sodium 252mg; Carbs 31.6g; Fiber 0.9g; Sugar 6.6g; Protein 3.7g

Pumpkin Muffins

Prep time: 20 minutes | **Cook time:** 20 minutes | **Serves:** 4

Ingredients:

- 1½ cups all-purpose flour
- ½ teaspoon baking soda
- ½ teaspoon baking powder
- 1 and ¼ teaspoons cinnamon, groaned
- ¼ teaspoon ground nutmeg, grated
- 2 large eggs
- Salt, pinch
- ¾ cup granulated sugar
- ½ cup dark brown sugar
- 1½ cups pumpkin puree
- ¼ cup coconut milk

Directions:

1. Take 4 ramekins and layer them with muffin paper.
2. In a bowl, add the eggs, brown sugar, baking soda, baking powder, cinnamon, nutmeg, and sugar and whisk well with an electric mixer.
3. In a second bowl, mix the flour, and salt.
4. Slowly add the dry Ingredients: to the wet Ingredients.
5. Fold in the pumpkin puree and milk and mix it in well.
6. Divide this batter into 4 ramekins.
7. Place two ramekins in each air fryer basket.
8. Set the time for zone 1 to 18 minutes at 360 degrees on AIR FRY mode.
9. Select the MATCH button for the zone 2 basket.
10. Check after the time is up and if not done, and let it AIR FRY for one more minute.
11. Once it is done, serve.

Serving Suggestion: Serve it with a glass of milk.

Variation Tip: Use almond milk instead of coconut milk.

Per Serving: Calories 291; Fat 6.4g; Sodium 241mg; Carbs 57.1g; Fiber 4.4g; Sugar 42g; Protein 5.9g

Chocolate Chip Muffins

Prep time: 12 minutes | **Cook time:** 15 minutes | **Serves:** 2

Ingredients:

- Salt, pinch
- 2 eggs
- ⅓ cup brown sugar
- ⅓ cup butter
- 4 tablespoons milk
- ¼ teaspoon vanilla extract
- ½ teaspoon baking powder
- 1 cup all-purpose flour
- 1 pouch chocolate chips, 35 grams

Directions:

1. Take 4 oven-safe ramekins that are the size of a cup and layer them with muffin papers.

2. In a bowl, with an electric beater mix the eggs, brown sugar, butter, milk, and vanilla extract.
3. In another bowl, mix the flour, baking powder, and salt.
4. Mix the dry Ingredients: into the wet Ingredients: slowly.
5. Fold in the chocolate chips and mix them in well.
6. Divide this batter into 4 ramekins and place them into both the baskets.
7. Set the time for zone 1 to 15 minutes at 350 degrees F on AIR FRY mode.
8. Select the MATCH button for the zone 2 basket.
9. If they are not completely done after 15 minutes, AIR FRY for another minute.
10. Once it is done, serve.

Serving Suggestion: Serve it with chocolate syrup drizzle

Variation Tip: None

Per Serving: Calories 757; Fat 40.3g; Sodium 426mg; Carbs 85.4g; Fiber 2.2g; Sugar 30.4g; Protein 14.4g

Apple Crisp

Prep time: 15 minutes| **Cook time:** 14 minutes | **Serves:** 8

Ingredients:

- 3 cups apples, chopped
- 1 tablespoon pure maple syrup
- 2 teaspoons lemon juice
- 3 tablespoons all-purpose flour
- ⅓ cup quick oats
- ¼ cup brown sugar
- 2 tablespoons light butter, melted
- ½ teaspoon cinnamon

Directions:

1. Toss the chopped apples with 1 tablespoon of all-purpose flour, cinnamon, maple syrup, and lemon juice in a suitable bowl.
2. Divide the apples in the two air fryer baskets with their crisper plates.
3. Whisk oats, brown sugar, and remaining all-purpose flour in a small bowl.
4. Stir in melted butter, then divide this mixture over the apples.
5. Return the crisper plate to the Ninja Foodi 2-Basket Air Fryer.
6. Select the Bake mode for Zone 1 and set the temperature to 375 degrees F and the time to 14 minutes.
7. Select the "MATCH" button to copy the settings for Zone 2.
8. Initiate cooking by pressing the START/STOP button.
9. Enjoy fresh.

Serving Suggestion: Serve with a warming cup of hot chocolate.

Variation Tip: Use crushed cookies or graham crackers instead of oats.

Per Serving: Calories 258; Fat 12.4g; Sodium 79mg; Carbs 34.3g; Fiber 1g; Sugar 17g; Protein 3.2g

Zesty Cranberry Scones

Prep time: 10 minutes | **Cook time:** 16 minutes | **Serves:** 8

Ingredients:

- 4 cups of flour
- ½ cup brown sugar
- 2 tablespoons baking powder
- ½ teaspoon ground nutmeg
- ½ teaspoon salt
- ½ cup butter, chilled and diced
- 2 cups fresh cranberry
- ⅔ cup sugar
- 2 tablespoons orange zest
- 1 ¼ cups half and half cream
- 2 eggs

Directions:

1. Whisk flour with baking powder, salt, nutmeg, and both the sugars in a bowl.
2. Stir in egg and cream, mix well to form a smooth dough.
3. Fold in cranberries along with the orange zest.
4. Knead this dough well on a work surface.
5. Cut 3-inch circles out of the dough.
6. Divide the scones in the crisper plates and spray them with cooking oil.
7. Return the crisper plates to the Ninja Foodi 2-Basket Air Fryer.
8. Choose the Air Fry mode for Zone 1 and set the temperature to 375 degrees F and the time to 16 minutes.
9. Select the "MATCH" button to copy the settings for Zone 2.
10. Initiate cooking by pressing the START/STOP button.
11. Flip the scones once cooked halfway and resume cooking.
12. Enjoy!

Serving Suggestion: Serve with cranberry jam on the side.

Variation Tip: Add raisins instead of cranberries to the dough.

Per Serving: Calories 204; Fat 9g; Sodium 91mg; Carbs 27g; Fiber 2.4g; Sugar 15g; Protein 1.3g

4-Week Meal Plan

Week 1

Monday

Breakfast: Bacon and Egg Omelet

Lunch: Air Fried Okra

Snack: Onion Rings

Dinner: Turkey and Beef Meatballs

Dessert: Apple Hand Pies

Tuesday

Breakfast: Yellow Potatoes with Eggs

Lunch: Brussels Sprouts

Snack: Potato Tater Tots

Dinner: Cheddar-Stuffed Chicken

Dessert: Fudge Brownies

Wednesday

Breakfast: Pumpkin Muffins

Lunch: Zucchini with Stuffing

Snack: Parmesan French Fries

Dinner: Smoked Salmon

Dessert: Chocolate Chip Muffins

Thursday

Breakfast: Seafood Shrimp Omelet

Lunch: Green Beans with Baked Potatoes

Snack: Chicken Tenders

Dinner: Savory Salmon Fillets

Dessert: Chocolate Chip Cake

Friday

Breakfast: Cinnamon Toasts

Lunch: Lime Glazed Tofu

Snack: Stuffed Bell Peppers

Dinner: Salmon with Coconut

Dessert: Zesty Cranberry Scones

Saturday

Breakfast: Banana and Raisins Muffins

Lunch: Quinoa Patties

Snack: Parmesan French Fries

Dinner: Crusted Shrimp

Dessert: Lemony Sweet Twists

Sunday

Breakfast: Morning Patties

Lunch: Kale and Spinach Chips

Snack: Dijon Cheese Sandwich

Dinner: General Tso's Chicken

Dessert: Fudge Brownies

Week 2

Monday:

Breakfast: Sweet Potatoes Hash

Lunch: Chicken Potatoes

Snack: Strawberries and Walnuts Muffins

Dinner: Beef Ribs II

Dessert: Chocolate Chip Cake

Tuesday

Breakfast: Banana and Raisins Muffins

Lunch: Brussels Sprouts

Snack: Chicken Crescent Wraps

Dinner: Spicy Lamb Chops

Dessert: Mini Blueberry Pies

Wednesday

Breakfast: Breakfast Casserole

Lunch: Falafel

Snack: Stuffed Bell Peppers

Dinner: Glazed Steak Recipe

Dessert: Zesty Cranberry Scones

Thursday

Breakfast: Breakfast Bacon

Lunch: Kale and Spinach Chips

Snack: Blueberries Muffins

Dinner: Short Ribs & Root Vegetables

Dessert: Apple Hand Pies

Friday

Breakfast: Yellow Potatoes with Eggs

Lunch: Brussels Sprouts

Snack: Potato Tater Tots

Dinner: Chipotle Beef

Dessert: Lemony Sweet Twists

Saturday

Breakfast: Sweet Potatoes Hash

Lunch: Quinoa Patties

Snack: Spicy Chicken Tenders

Dinner: Zucchini Pork Skewers

Dessert: Biscuit Doughnuts

Sunday

Breakfast: Banana and Raisins Muffins

Lunch: Green Beans with Baked Potatoes

Snack: Strawberries and Walnuts Muffins

Dinner: Pork Chops

Dessert: Mini Blueberry Pies

Week 3

Monday:

Breakfast: Morning Patties

Lunch: Fried Artichoke Hearts

Snack: Spicy Chicken Tenders

Dinner: Gochujang Brisket

Dessert: Chocolate Chip Cake

Tuesday

Breakfast: Bacon and Egg Omelet

Lunch: Quinoa Patties

Snack: Chicken Crescent Wraps

Dinner: Chicken Breast Strips

Dessert: Biscuit Doughnuts

Wednesday

Breakfast: Breakfast Casserole

Lunch: Kale and Spinach Chips

Snack: Potato Tater Tots

Dinner: Fried Lobster Tails

Dessert: Pumpkin Muffins

Thursday

Breakfast: Bacon and Egg Omelet

Lunch: Zucchini with Stuffing

Snack: Cheddar Quiche

Dinner: Savory Salmon Fillets

Dessert: Air Fryer Sweet Twists

Friday

Breakfast: Morning Patties

Lunch: Lime Glazed Tofu

Snack: Onion Rings

Dinner: Salmon with Green Beans

Dessert: Fudge Brownies

Saturday

Breakfast: Bacon and Egg Omelet

Lunch: Seafood Shrimp Omelet

Snack: Blueberries Muffins

Dinner: Chinese BBQ Pork

Dessert: Walnuts Fritters

Sunday

Breakfast: Pumpkin Muffins

Lunch: Salmon with Fennel Salad

Snack: Parmesan French Fries

Dinner: Air Fryer Meatloaves

Dessert: Zesty Cranberry Scones

Week 4

Monday:

Breakfast: Seafood Shrimp Omelet

Lunch: Stuffed Tomatoes

Snack: Spicy Chicken Tenders

Dinner: Turkey and Beef Meatballs

Dessert: Lemony Sweet Twists

Tuesday

Breakfast: Egg with Baby Spinach

Lunch: Kale and Spinach Chips

Snack: Chicken Crescent Wraps

Dinner: Spicy Lamb Chops

Dessert: Mini Blueberry Pies

Wednesday

Breakfast: Banana and Raisins Muffins

Lunch: Fried Artichoke Hearts

Snack: Peppered Asparagus

Dinner: Beef & Broccoli

Dessert: Chocolate Chip Cake

Thursday

Breakfast: Bacon and Egg Omelet

Lunch: Air Fried Okra

Snack: Strawberries and Walnuts Muffins

Dinner: Crumbed Chicken Katsu

Dessert: Apple Crisp

Friday

Breakfast: Cinnamon Toasts

Lunch: Lime Glazed Tofu

Snack: Chicken Crescent Wraps

Dinner: Air Fried Turkey Breast

Dessert: Chocolate Chip Muffins

Saturday

Breakfast: Sweet Potatoes Hash

Lunch: Brussels Sprouts

Snack: Potato Tater Tots

Dinner: Balsamic Duck Breast

Dessert: Fudge Brownies

Sunday

Breakfast: Pumpkin Muffins

Lunch: Salmon with Fennel Salad

Snack: Spicy Chicken Tenders

Dinner: General Tso's Chicken

Dessert: Walnuts Fritters

Conclusion

Isn't it straightforward to cook supper in your Ninja Foodi 2-Basket Air Fryer? The smart air fryer has two zones to cook different meals at once. It is now possible to cook with a superior disposition. The air fryer will fit around the dish you're cooking, and that's a great magic to get a 5-star rating. Another good thing is that it's a relatively inexpensive product. The only thing the user has to do before using this appliance is just to check what food it can cook. It is very beneficial for health, especially for people with certain health conditions. It's time to get cooking with the Ninja Foodi 2-Basket Air Fryer.

© Copyright 2021 –
All rights reserved

This document is geared towards providing exact and reliable information with regards to the topic and issue covered. The publication is sold with the idea that the publisher is not required to render accounting, officially permitted, or otherwise, qualified services. If advice is necessary, legal, or professional, a practiced individual in the profession should be ordered. -From a Declaration of Principles which was accepted and approved equally by a Committee of the American Bar Association and a Committee of Publishers and Associations. In no way is it legal to reproduce, duplicate, or transmit any part of this document in either electronic means or in printed format. Recording of this publication is strictly prohibited and any storage of this document is not allowed unless with written permission from the publisher.

All rights reserved. The information provided herein is stated to be truthful and consistent, in that any liability, in terms of inattention or otherwise, by any usage or abuse of any policies, processes, or Directions: contained within is the solitary and utter responsibility of the recipient reader.

Under no circumstances will any legal responsibility or blame be held against the publisher for any reparation, damages, or monetary loss due to the information herein, either directly or indirectly. Respective authors own all copyrights not held by the publisher.

The information herein is offered for informational purposes solely, and is universal as

so. The presentation of the information is without contract or any type of guarantee assurance. The trademarks that are used are without any consent, and the publication of the trademark is without permission or backing by the trademark owner.

All trademarks and brands within this book are for clarifying purposes only and are the owned by the owners themselves, not affiliated with this document.

Printed in Great Britain
by Amazon